fro

see page 101

Basking

in

His Presence

Basking
In
His Presence

A Call to the
Prayer of Silence

Bill Volkman

UNION
LIFE

1996
Union Life Ministries
675 Roosevelt Road
Glen Ellyn, Illinois, 60137

Copyright © 1996 Bill Volkman

First Edition—1996
Dickinson Press, Grand Rapids, Michigan

COVER PHOTO: *Bridgeman/Art Resource, New York, New York.* CHRIST IN THE HOUSE OF MARY AND MARTHA, *by Jan Vermeer (1632-1675 A.D.), National Gallery of Scotland, Edinburgh, Scotland, U.K.*

LITHOGRAPH: CHRIST IN THE HOUSE OF MARY AND MARTHA, *by Miradzhki* *Pinx, 1886 A.D.*

Library of Congress Cataloging-in-Publication Data

Volkman, Bill, 1925—

ISBN 1-889870-08-0

DEDICATION

To my thirteen precious grandchildren: Valerie, Brian, Adam, Shawn, Steve, Lisa, Lindsey, Brett, Katie, Andy, Matt, Bill and Scott—each of whom has taught me much about the greatest thing in the world: love.

My heart's desire is that each of them, in due season, will find the fulfillment and the rest in life that only a love affair with God brings—that they will taste the sweetness of their relationship with the Lover within them.

SPECIAL ACKNOWLEDGMENTS

To Richard Zenith—who took time out of his busy writing, translating and editing schedule in Portugal to once again perform a miracle on what might otherwise have been a very mediocre manuscript.

To Jan Ord—who first suffered through the trauma of teaching an old dog the tricks of using a word processor (which proved invaluable!), and then spent countless hours editing with me and making all the preparations for publication.

To Jeannette and Stan Bakke, Bruce Johnson and my daughter-in-law Claudia Volkman—who each edited my total manuscript twice, coming up with numerous helpful suggestions, as well as encouraging me through the whole process.

To Gary Bonikowsky, Laurie Hills, Steve Pettit, Burt Rosenberg, Julie Steenson, Dan Stone and John Whittle—all of whom read the first draft and gave me wise counsel.

To Marge—my wife of 51 years, my life-partner on this journey of discovery, who has faithfully stood by me and cared enough to listen and wait as I tried to sort out what God was showing me; not to mention her help in reading the innumerable drafts of this manuscript during the past year. Thank you, Dove, for your faithfulness and love.

CONTENTS

PREFACE 11

1   A MAJOR TURNING POINT 15

2   "COME TO ME" 25

3   "BEHOLD I STAND AT THE DOOR" 35

4   BASKING IN HIS PRESENCE 43

5   FROM COMPULSIVENESS TO CONTENTMENT 51

6   THE RESIDENT PSYCHOTHERAPIST 59

7   UNCONDITIONAL LOVE 69

8   ANOTHER LIFE-CHANGING ENCOUNTER 79

9   LOOKING AT THE HEART 89

10   INTENTION AND ATTENTION 97

11   THE TREE OF UNKNOWING 105

12   DISCOVERING OUR DESTINY IN ADVERSITY 115

13   IT'S ALL VERY SIMPLE 125

14   THE PRECIOUSNESS OF THE PRESENT MOMENT 135

EPILOGUE 147

Now as they were traveling along, Jesus entered a certain village; and a woman named Martha welcomed Him into her home.

And she had a sister called Mary, who moreover was listening to the Lord's word, seated at His feet.

But Martha was distracted with all her preparations; and she came up to Him, and said, "Lord, do You not care that my sister has left me to do all the serving alone? Then tell her to help me."

But the Lord answered and said to her, "Martha, Martha, you are worried and bothered about so many things; but only a few things are necessary, really only one, for Mary has chosen the good part, which shall not be taken from her."

Luke 10:38-42

The custodian of a church had the responsibility of unlocking the doors at six o'clock each morning. On weekdays, his other duties were to tend to the necessary cleaning and maintenance of the church building and grounds.

Only occasionally did he see a parishioner enter the sanctuary for a few moments of meditation and prayer. One day he realized that each morning an elderly woman, obviously of modest means, quietly entered the church a few minutes after he opened the front doors. She always sat in the back pew. And she unobtrusively slipped out of the church about two hours later.

After observing her for many months, the custodian, unable to contain his curiosity any longer, timidly approached the woman. He said, "Pardon me, Madam, may I ask you a question?"

She smiled her assent.

"I have watched you come in here day after day, sit quietly in the same pew, and then walk out two hours later. What are you doing?"

She replied matter-of-factly: "I look at Him, He looks at me, we look at each other."

PREFACE

Basking in His Presence is an update of my spiritual pilgrimage since writing *The Wink of Faith* in 1983. It's a call to the prayer of silence. It's a call to practice contemplative prayer and to experience the contemplative life. It's a call to be still, to turn within, to come home. It's a call to "transforming union"; to experiential union; to an intimate, on-going love affair with our indwelling Lover. Yes, it's a call to experience the ecstasy of being in love with our Beloved.

The positive response I received to *The Wink of Faith* was most gratifying. Soon after it was published, many readers wrote or called to tell me how much *The Wink* had helped them to come to a new recognition of who they are in Christ. But with the accolades, I also heard a lot of people asking: "Now that I know who the 'real me' is, why is my life still messed up? Why can't I better handle the overwhelming temptations and tensions of everyday life?"

So, wanting to answer these questions, I soon started a second book, which I planned to entitle, *Turning Tensions into Triumph*. But I quickly found out that I wasn't ready to write such a book about effectively living the Christian life, because I didn't have an adequate answer for my own life! I knew a lot of theory, but experiential love, joy and peace were still eluding me.

I had to spend ten more years on my own spiritual pilgrimage before I would try once again to tackle the questions my readers had asked. Like Job, I had some answers and knew a lot about God, but I had not yet seen Him with the transforming single eye of faith.

I almost entitled this book, "Life Begins at 65," as it wasn't until I was age 65 that God opened my eyes to see my smallness and His greatness. Again, like Job, for most of my life I hadn't had a clue about the extent of my spiritual poverty and desperate need of inner healing and transformation, nor did I understand God's passionate love for me.

Though I hesitate to compare myself in any way with St. Augustine, I feel I can echo his observation about his personal slowness in responding to God's persistent call:

> *Late have I loved You, O beauty so ancient and so new!*
> *Late have I loved You. Behold You were ever within me,*
> *and I abroad, seeking You there. I...rushed madly about*
> *in the midst of forms beautiful which You had made. You*
> *were ever with me, but I was not with You. The very*
> *things which had not been, unless they were in You, kept*
> *me from You. You called me by name, You cried aloud*
> *to me, and Your voice pierced my deafness.*
> *The Confessions, Book X, Chapter 27*

Life is a call to "be." It is a call to forget separated self, and to become totally lost in our God. Our focus must shift from what we get out of life to offering ourselves as a gift to our Lover.

Look at the picture of Mary, Martha and Jesus on the cover of this book. Why wasn't Mary paying any attention to what Martha was doing? Because she was lost in her beloved Lord. Mary wasn't thinking about what she could do for Jesus, or what He could do for her. She was completely absorbed in her love for Him and in His unconditional love of her.

Mary's behavior might seem radical, but she was right. And it's high time that we shift gears and lose ourselves in the Beloved. Let's stop spending all our time learning "about" God and "working for" Him. Let's spend some of that time practicing His presence and just adoring Him.

If anyone asked me for a single practical suggestion for living the Christian life, this is what I would tell them. Experience the prayer of silence—wordless prayer. Practice contemplative prayer. Don't just read, talk about and analyze it. Faithfully practice basking in God's presence in solitude and silence twice a day for ten minutes for thirty days. If you do this—with loving God and being attentive to His presence as your primary goal—you will never be the same. And chances are that you will be a practicing contemplative for the rest of your life.

1

A MAJOR
TURNING POINT

Your way to God begins on the day of your conversion, for conversion marks your soul's initial return to God. From that moment you begin to live and have your being by the means of His grace. After your conversion, your own spirit—the human spirit (which is deep within your inmost being)—is touched by God and is made alive and functioning.

Your spirit, in turn, invites your soul to compose itself and to turn within, there to find the God who has newly come to reside at the center of your being. Your spirit instructs your soul that, since God is more present deep within you, He cannot be found anywhere else. Henceforth, He must be sought within. And He must be enjoyed there, alone.

Therefore, from the very beginning, you find great joy in knowing that your Lord is within you and that you can find Him and enjoy Him in your inmost being. From the very beginning of your conversion it is possible for you to know, from the very outset of your life in Christ, that what you are to pursue is that inward life.

—*Jeanne Guyon*

1

A MAJOR
TURNING POINT

One Sunday afternoon in the summer of 1990 I received a phone call from my son, Scott. The one-sided conversation in response to my "Hello" went something like this: "Dad, turn on Channel 11. There's this guy on TV who you've got to hear!" *Click!* Scott had hung up.

Obediently, I turned on our TV. The speaker who Scott was so anxious for me to hear was the psychologist John Bradshaw, a well-known lecturer and author. His subject was *dysfunctionality*. And I didn't even really know what the word meant!

PBS was in the middle of its semi-annual fund-raising drive, so it was rerunning some of its best programs. It had scheduled five of Bradshaw's 50-minute lectures for that Sunday afternoon, with another five scheduled for the following Sunday.

It was Scott's phone call which initiated what was to be *the* watershed experience of my life. My journey of faith has been marked by a number of life-changing events, but it was at age 65 that God engineered the most significant turning point.

My wife, Marge, and I didn't have to listen to Bradshaw for very long before we understood why Scott insisted

17

that we tune in. He was bluntly pointing out that most of us grow up as dysfunctional persons, and that most of us continue to operate with substantial dysfunctionality for the rest of our lives. Bradshaw's observations and illustrations that afternoon were like a bombshell to me. They seemed to specifically address issues which I had conveniently, though unwittingly, ignored for a lifetime.

During each of the long fund-raising breaks between lectures, Scott and I enthusiastically shared by phone the various points that hit home for each of us. We reflected on some of the episodes that occurred between us while Scott was growing up, as well as some of my personal experiences during my childhood.

Bradshaw emphasized that from early on in life we are all wounded and traumatized, to some extent, by our parents, relatives, teachers, peers and others who touch our lives as we're growing up. Instead of being consistently affirmed as persons, we are often disaffirmed and judged, in a thousand different ways. Who knows the extent of the damage that can be caused by such treatment in our formative years.

None of us has come away unscathed from the countless incidents of minor physical and/or verbal abuse that we are subjected to in childhood. In most cases, those who had a part in raising us were far from mature, fully-functioning adults, and their inconsistent and sometimes angry and harmful treatment of us naturally produced another generation of dysfunctional persons.

I hope no one takes offense because I label us, our parents, and just about everyone else as dysfunctional. By my strict definition, a "dysfunctional person" is any person who does not function as a whole person 100% of the time. That obviously includes all of us. We all have our share of inordinate fears, guilt, blind spots, areas of denial, needs to be affirmed, compulsiveness, and other eccentricities. We all continue to need a measure of inner healing and progressive transformation. For all humanity, spiritual and emotional growth turns out to be a lifelong pilgrimage.

Marge and I found each of Bradshaw's sessions to be both revealing and challenging. Personally, it seemed as if all of his illustrations were given with me in mind. Again and again I found myself saying to Marge, "That's me he's talking about!" Seven years after writing *The Wink of Faith,* and fifteen years after starting to publish *Union Life* magazine, I discovered that after all my years as a zealous Christian, I had only scratched the surface of being a new creation in Christ.

During the week between the two Sunday sessions, Scott, his wife Claudia, Marge and I talked among ourselves. We continued to share some of the episodes that Bradshaw had talked about and then compared them with some of the experiences, both positive and negative, that each of us had when we were younger. Bradshaw's comments had caused us to remember a lot of events that might well have been abusive and damaging to our psychological and spiritual growth.

By the time I'd heard most of Bradshaw's second five-hour series, I was totally devastated. During one of the last commercials I said to Marge: "You know, I'm messed up beyond imagination! What Bradshaw is talking about sure explains a lot of things for me. No wonder I've found love, joy and peace so elusive!"

I was looking forward to the last lecture, as Bradshaw had said that in that session he would tell us how we could deal with our dysfunctionalities and have them healed. I had hoped he would give a step-by-step remedy that I could follow. However, I was disappointed to hear that there was no easy solution. It was easier to point out the problem than it was to give a viable solution. Bradshaw's only concrete suggestions were to either join a 12-step program or get professional, psychological help.

Somehow, neither of his solutions seemed right for me.

Bradshaw's emphasis on the need for affirmation and affection during early childhood—together with his enlightening illustrations—had caused me to reflect seriously on a distant childhood which I had rarely thought about in recent years. In the weeks that followed, I continued to examine my personal experience and do some deep soul-searching.

Being raised by two good, hard-working German parents, my two brothers and I knew nothing but "performance." *Just do it*—no argument, no discussion, no explanation. Just do what you are told.

I faced into the fact that words of affirmation and displays of love and affection had been rare in our home. The first and last time I can remember my parents kissing me was when I was eighteen years old. As I was leaving to go into military service, to my surprise, they each kissed and hugged me goodbye.

But I wasn't being singled out. My parents didn't show any affection to my brothers or to each other either. I shared with Marge another significant memory that resurfaced as we talked. When my two brothers and I were quite young, our father made a trip back to his home town in Germany, leaving my mother to take care of us. Young as I was, I still remember thinking how strange it was that they simply shook hands when my dad left for his two-month visit to Europe!

My parents were strict Baptists. On Sundays, the five of us piled into the car morning and evening to attend all services at a German Baptist church. The other six days we had devotions at 6 A.M. around our dining room table. Aunt Gretchen (one of my mother's sisters) lived in an apartment upstairs and joined us each morning for Bible reading and prayer. In keeping with how seriously they took their faith, the devotions were pretty somber most of the time. But added to that was the chilling, negative atmosphere between my dad and my aunt, who had an on-going feud for as long as I can remember, rarely speaking to each other. To break the tension, we three boys giggled and horsed around under the table while we waited impatiently on our knees during prayer time.

I can remember, as a little boy, hearing my dad speaking in his quaint, German-accented English, as he told whoever would listen about his conversion experience. It was at Mother Remus' boarding house in the suburbs of Chicago, not long after immigrating to America, that my father accepted Christ as his personal Savior. My dad was still giving the same testimony in church fifty years later.

My mother was always the teacher of the women's Sunday School class at our church. All I can remember is that I resented her spending so many hours preparing for her classes, especially those on her favorite books— Ezekiel, Daniel and Revelation. I still don't understand her great fascination with end times—the "moving wheels" in Ezekiel, the "70 weeks" in the book of Daniel, and the "whore of Babylon," the "24 elders," the "six seals," and the "six trumpets" in the book of Revelation.

At one point Marge asked me, "Can't you think of any fun times you had with your folks? Didn't they ever talk to you, laugh with you and affirm you?"

I thought for a long time. Finally I said, "Yes, I can remember one time, with my Mom." So I related the following episode.

At about age 11, I was in the bathroom combing my hair. My older brother, Wally, came in, looked at me and said, "You sure are ugly. Why do you put all that grease in your hair and slick it straight back like that? Why don't you at least put a little wave in it—like this?" With brotherly disdain, he proceeded to show me what he meant.

"Leave me alone!" I bellowed. My mother, who was in

the kitchen, heard me and could tell I was on the verge of tears. So she called me and sat me down at the kitchen table. She said, "Don't listen to your brother. Listen to me. Some day in the future your cheeks will fill out and you will grow up to be a handsome young man!" I never forgot those rare words of affirmation. Her prophecy didn't prove to be quite accurate—the only thing that filled out was my waistline—but they were important words of encouragement at the time.

As I reflected on all my childhood memories, I kept asking myself the same question: *Could the lack of affection and affirmation on the part of my parents have been the main cause of my continuing dysfunctionality through the years?* I didn't know the answer to that question, but I did know that I wasn't interested in blaming my dead parents for my failure to grow up to be a whole, balanced, responsible person.

At age 65, I was prepared to be honest. I had finally recognized that I was *anything* but a whole, balanced, responsible person. In spite of forty years of good intentions and sacrificial involvement in countless ministries and lives, I still knew down deep that I was a failure. Though I had learned something through the years—I was much more loving and affirming as a grandparent than I had been as a parent—I realized that, though well-intentioned, my autocratic, dogmatic, aggressive approach to life had hurt a lot of people through the years, beginning with my wife and children.

Many years ago, the pastor of a Baptist church where I was very active said to me, "Bill, can't I do anything to please you?" I don't recall the circumstances that precipitated his remark, but the memory of the anguish in his eyes and in his voice still haunts me. He was a humble, caring man of God, so I couldn't discount his observation. Unfortunately, it would be many more years before I would recognize the depth of my problems, and find that my solution for them had been available all along.

Bradshaw's lectures and my subsequent reflections convinced me of one thing: the fruit of the Spirit, starting with love, joy and peace, and ending with self-control, were all in short supply in my life.

So I took the matter to the Lord. "Lord, I'm 65, and I still don't seem to know anything about loving, about being loved, about joy, rest and contentment, or anything else that's really important. But I don't care to get into the blame-game or dredge up who did what to make me end up being such a mess. And I'm not going to pay some shrink a hundred bucks a session for the rest of my life to help me sort all this out. If I'm going to be healed and transformed, it's up to You to do it—in Your way and by Your timetable."

A couple of weeks later, a colleague gave me a book she said I *had* to read. It was Thomas Keating's *Open Mind, Open Heart*, a book on contemplative prayer. One sentence in the ninth chapter, "The Unloading of the Unconscious," turned out to be my *Magna Carta* to freedom. Keating wrote, "If you are faithful to the daily practice of contemplative prayer, your psychic wounds will be healed without your being re-traumatized." The words "without your being re-traumatized" screamed out at me. I was glad to hear that I did not have to relive all the painful events of the past in order to be made whole.

Keating's pointed answer to inner wounds and their resulting dysfunctionality was *centering*, or *contemplative prayer*. His advice to his readers: learn to wait on God in silence, learn to practice His presence, learn to rest in faith in Him, learn to just *be* unto God. For a few minutes, perhaps twice a day, stop all the words and analyses, and just "come home" to the inner center of your being, where your human spirit is one with the indwelling Spirit of Christ.

I took Keating's advice. From that day on I started the faith-practice of contemplative prayer and I have consistently practiced it to this day. From that day on I have looked to the Christ within as my Resident Psychotherapist, as my only hope of healing, transformation and divinization. I have also attempted to come to Him just for Himself, without any expectations, without an agenda; and to see myself as a gift that I give to God.

By God's grace and intervention, my seventeen-year focus on *union* was to significantly shift to a focus on *union for communion*. My *union* (knowing about union) was to finally become *union life; positional union* was to move to *experiential union*. The result is that the promised fruit of the Spirit—love, joy, peace, etc.—is gradually becoming an experienced reality in my life.

2

"COME TO ME"

In recent years, I seem to hear God say, "Put your books away and just be with Me. Trust your experience. There are no experts in prayer, only people who have been faithful to the ache in their hearts."

I reflect on this with both anxiety and joy. Why shouldn't our experiences be filled with God? Who do we think it is who is breathing in us? Where do we think this ache has come from? And has it ever crossed your mind that God, too, has a fierce ache for you? This is the only message I've been getting in prayer these days: "Forget the experts for a while. Trust your own experience."

You are the dwelling place for the source of All Life. You are an offspring of the One who said, "I am who I am." If the One who gave you birth lives within you, surely you can find some resources there in your sacred Center.

An expert lives within you. An expert breathes out of you. Are you able to be still enough to become intimate with the One who lives within? He is the only expert you will ever meet. Your life is entwined with the God who gave you birth.

Frail dust, remember, you are splendor!

—*Macrina Wiederkehr*

2

"COME TO ME"

Throughout my childhood in the suburbs of Chicago, my family attended church whenever the doors were open. It was a beautiful old building with three huge stained-glass windows—one on each side of the sanctuary and one over the choir loft.

Being German immigrants, my parents had joined a German Baptist church with a bilingual pastor. He conducted the first service in German, which was followed by Sunday School and the main service in English. Even though I and my two brothers knew very little German, we had to go to both worship services, as well as Sunday School.

One Sunday morning, when we were about eight years old, my twin brother, Ernie, and I were challenged by our Sunday School teacher with these words: "I want to find out how many of you guys are good detectives. This morning, when you go to church, I want you to carefully examine the stained-glass window on the south wall of the sanctuary—it's the one on the left side as you face the pulpit."

Our teacher continued: "It's a picture of Jesus gently knocking on a door with His right hand. The artist who designed that window left something out, and I want you to figure out what it is. Let's see how many of you can identify what is wrong with that picture and share it with us next Sunday morning in class."

As Ernie and I went into the sanctuary with our older brother, Wally, and our parents, we steered the family into a pew as close as possible to the stained-glass window in question. We then played detective, examining the picture in detail and whispering our conclusions to each other. But, as hard as we looked, we couldn't figure out the artist's "mistake."

As we were heading home from church, we told our mother about our assignment. Her response surprised both of us. She laughed—which didn't happen very often—and she was able to tell us the answer.

Mom said, "Boys, that artist didn't make a mistake. He knew exactly what he was doing. He got his idea for that stained-glass window from the Bible where it says: 'Behold, I stand at the door and knock; if anyone hears My voice and opens the door, I will come in to him, and will dine with him, and he with Me.'

"What does every door have? That's right—a handle on each side, so that the door can be opened from inside or outside. But this artist purposely left the handle off the outside. You see, it's supposed to be a picture of a door that each of us has in our heart. Jesus wants to come into each of our lives, but He's a gentleman and will never force His way in. It's up to us to open the door from the inside."

I don't really remember any more of the details of what was said, but I do know my mom talked some more to me about all of this after dinner. It was on that Sunday afternoon that I made the decision to open my heart's door and invite Jesus into my life. This was my conversion experience—what we called being "born again."

A couple of years later, when I was about ten years old, that same Sunday School teacher gave us another challenge—this time to memorize Scripture. He gave each of us a list of 26 Bible verses *(KJV)*—one for each of the 26 letters of the alphabet. There was to be a small prize for every five verses we memorized, and then a grand prize for anyone who learned all 26 verses.

Being analytical, one of the first things I did was to look at the end of the mimeographed list to see what verses my teacher had been able to find beginning with "X" and with "Z."

It bothered me that for "X" he chose John 3:3—"Except a man be born again...." That was almost like cheating. Not only did the verse not begin with an "X," it didn't actually even begin with the word "Except"! The part we were to memorize was only the last half of the verse.

His verse for the letter "Z" was Luke 19:8: "And Zaccheus stood...." That also bothered me because the verse began with the word "And," not with a word starting with the letter "Z." At ten years old I was already a Bible literalist and legalist, more concerned about technicalities than real substance!

Even though I had set out to learn all 26 verses, I ended up learning only ten, and therefore got only two small prizes. But the teacher's goal was still achieved—I had memorized some verses that I would never forget.

After all these years I can still recite the first three verses. The "A" verse was Isaiah 53:6—"All we like sheep have gone astray...." The "B" verse was Revelation 3:20—"Behold, I stand at the door, and knock...." The "C" verse was Matthew 11:28—"Come unto Me...and I will give you rest." As I look back now, I appreciate that Sunday School teacher a lot more than I did at the time. Those sure are important verses!

My mother had taught my two brothers and me from early on that the Bible is God's love-letter to us, and that it teaches us how to live the Christian life. She told us that God blesses those who "meditate on His Law day and night." So Biblical meditation—Bible reading, Bible study and Bible memorization—became an important part of my life as I grew up in the faith.

Without question, these habits brought me much spiritual growth and many blessings. In more recent years, however, I reflected on several familiar verses and began to wonder if I really understood what they meant.

One verse was John 5:39-40: "You search the Scriptures, because you think that in them you have eternal life...[but] you are unwilling to come to Me, that you may have life." Exactly what did Jesus mean when He said, "You are unwilling to come to Me that you may have life"? I had done plenty of searching of the Scriptures through the years, but now, looking back on my life, I see that I was always *looking to words* for life rather than *coming to Him* for life. I now know that "Life"—with a capital "L"—is a Person, not a place or a thing. That Person was calling me, and calls each of us, to come to Him in an intimate personal love relationship.

The second verse that haunted me was the "C" verse which I had memorized in my youth—"Come to Me, all who are weary and heavy laden, and I will give you rest." Verse 29 continues with the promise: "Take My yoke upon you, and learn from Me, for I am gentle and humble in heart; and you shall find rest for your souls."

"Rest for my *soul*"?! What's that? Since I was a boy I've always known rest in my *spirit*, but the truth is that at age 65 I still didn't know rest in my *soul*. I had known for decades that I was going to heaven, but I sure hadn't known how to live above the pressures of everyday life. Experiential rest had eluded me. Life was a chore rather than contentment. Exactly what did Jesus mean when He said, "Come unto Me"?

Within myself, I kept asking this question: *Is my present experience really all there is to the promise of "abundant life"? Am I still missing something?* As recently as a couple of years ago—imagine, after fifteen years as Editor of *Union*

30

Life, knowing and sharing the liberating message of our union with Christ with countless people around the world—I still felt that something was missing. I knew that somehow there had to be a level of inner rest, joy, victory, and outflowing love that went far beyond my erratic everyday experience.

Where was *my* "Sabbath rest"? Where was *my* "joy unspeakable"? Why didn't *I* "overwhelmingly conquer"? Why didn't *I* demonstrate "unconditional love"? Where was the "fruit of the Spirit"? What was it that I was still missing?

I know now that I still had to discover that there was a more intimate aspect to my union with Christ than simply knowing about it. My *positional* union had to become an *experiential* union. I had to learn to *come to Him* in an on-going love relationship. I had to learn that God's *passionate desire* is a loving intimacy with each one of us. Life is much more than doing; it's *being*. Life is *being in love* with God.

And now that I have begun to experience something of this loving intimacy, a large measure of the long anticipated and sought-after fruit—love, joy, peace and even rest—has finally come! Thomas Keating was right. My daily faith-practice of "centering," or contemplative prayer, has brought an unimagined level of inner healing and transformation.

At last I have learned something of what Jesus meant when He said, "Come to Me"—what it means to come home to the Christ who lives at the center of my being. Now I take time daily to be lovingly attentive to the Christ with whom I am in union. I take time for inner listening and waiting on God, as well as for outer study, prayer and praise. I practice both contemplation and meditation. And it's this time with Him—when I am not thinking about anything, not doing anything, just being with Him—that is the sweetest time of all.

Contemplation is not the same thing as meditation. The latter is discursive—it's talking, thinking, reading, analyzing, studying. Contemplation is the absence of all these things; it's simply being. It doesn't matter whether we call it "practicing the Presence," "centering," "basking in His presence," or any one of a dozen other terms. What matters is that we experience it. There is a big difference between the information that flows from meditation, and the transformation that issues from contemplation. Whatever your past experience has been, consider whether you shouldn't take some time daily to "be still," to quietly wait in silence on the Holy Spirit at your center.

Centering has brought about an unbelievable transformation in the way I see things, as well as in the way I live out my life at home and in society. Transformation is what I needed, and what we all need continuously. But how are we to be transformed; how are we to be changed into the likeness of Christ?

In past years when I read the words of Romans 12:2— "And do not be conformed to this world, but be transformed by the renewing of your mind"—I mistakenly thought that the word "mind" was the same as "brain." I had failed to distinguish soul and spirit. I had wrongly assumed that inward transformation was something I could accomplish by filling my brain with Scriptural truths, concepts and principles.

But now I see that I needed a lot more than that. God means to transform us from the inside out. The renewing of our minds takes place in our inner being by the work of the *Living Word within*, not just by knowing the written Word.

This probably was why Paul says in Romans 10:8 that the word is very near us, in our mouths *and* in our hearts. Yes, liberation starts when we acknowledge our need, but inner transformation comes only through the work of the Living Word within us. God is calling us to come home, to come *to Him* at the center of our being, so that He can renew our minds and hearts from within by His indwelling Spirit.

If you have not yet found "rest for your soul," why would you resist Jesus' call to "Come unto Me"?

God's favorite dwelling place is within you! Try coming home to Him each day in a time of quiet contemplation. I think you will be amazed at the transformation and at the new level of love, joy and peace that will gradually become your experience as you are faithful to this practice.

3

"BEHOLD I STAND AT THE DOOR"

There are two kinds of solitude. There is an outward solitude when one simply does not speak, or speaks little. There is also an inner solitude. Inner solitude means forgetting about everything around you, being detached from it, surrendering all purpose and desire and thought and will, and then coming before the Lord.

This is true solitude. You will find it to be a sweet rest and an inward serenity, found only in the arms of your Lord. For that believer who is able to stay in such a place before his Lord there will be a great number of discoveries.

For the believer who comes this far there is the discovery that the Lord converses and communicates with the believer in his inward parts. It is in that place the Lord fills the believer with Himself, but fills him only because that person is empty. He clothes him with light and with love because he is naked, lifts him up because he is lowly, and unites him with God and transforms him, because he is alone.

I see this solitude with God as a figure of eternal bliss—a picture of that future time when the eternal Father will be forever beheld.

—*Michael Molinos*

Mr Rhoda Oberholtzer

To alice Lapp -
for the Church Library

Rhoda

ANGEL TREE.

For more information about Angel Tree,
visit us online at www.angeltree.org
or call us at 1-800-55-ANGEL.

3

"BEHOLD I STAND
AT THE DOOR"

When Marge and I visited St. Paul's Cathedral in London in 1995, we saw for the first time Holman Hunt's famous painting, *The Light of the World*. It depicts Jesus with a lamp in His left hand, knocking on a vine-covered plank door. This is probably the most celebrated Victorian religious painting in the world. It exists in three versions—each painted by Hunt, over a 50-year time-span—the last and largest of which hangs in St. Paul's.

In large, all-cap letters, in the lower part of the picture's massive, gold-etched frame, Hunt had engraved the following words (taken from Revelation 3:20):

BEHOLD I STAND AT THE DOOR AND KNOCK
IF ANY MAN HEAR MY VOICE AND OPEN THE DOOR
I WILL COME INTO HIM AND WILL SUP WITH HIM
AND HE WITH ME.

Though we had been to St. Paul's before, somehow we had missed seeing this particular painting. Marge and I looked carefully at the painting, appreciating each detail. It had many similarities to the stained-glass window which was so instrumental in my conversion at the age of eight. My guess is that the artist who designed the stained-glass window in the church of my youth probably got his inspiration from Hunt's world-famous, *The Light of the World.*

As Marge and I talked about the meaning of the painting, we realized afresh how much our understanding of Revelation 3:20 has changed. We used to appreciate it as a verse addressed strictly to unbelievers, inviting them to accept Christ and the salvation He offers. Now we also see it as a continuing invitation to all Christians throughout their lives. It seems that most of us who have asked Jesus into our heart's home have relegated Him to some single room or closet. So He continues to knock on our heart's living-room, dining-room or bedroom door, desiring that we make and keep a tryst with Him each day.

We recently received a disheartening cancellation request from a *Union Life* subscriber. "I have been receiving your wonderful free magazine for over ten years now," wrote the subscriber, "but I can no longer receive it in good conscience. Claudia Volkman, in her editorial, wrote that Revelation 3:20, like many other Scriptures, 'has many layers of meaning.'

"Claudia added that she felt that it 'is Christ's invitation to us to dine with Him in loving intimacy and true communion.' But I do not feel that is what John meant when he wrote that verse. So please drop my name from your mailing list."

While we all have the right to our view of Scripture, it saddened me that this reader couldn't see the point that Claudia was making—that perhaps certain Scriptures do have a larger meaning than we first thought. This is what Claudia had written that prompted the cancellation:

> *Christ is not only offering to enter our hearts and take up residence; He is offering to dine with us.... But there is more. There is His invitation to us to answer His*

*deeper knocking at the inner recesses of our hearts. We
are meant to be, not do; we are meant to be in love. For
it is in this feast of love, which we are invited to daily,
even hourly, that we are truly equipped with the inner
resources necessary to be love to our world.*

During the earlier years of *Union Life* magazine, we
emphasized the mystery of the Gospel—Christ in us, the
hope of glory. We encouraged our readers to recognize
who they are in their union with Christ, so as to close the
perceived gap of separation between them and a "distant"
God. This emphasis is wonderful, but it is only a
beginning. "Union with Christ," like marriage, is not
meant to be theoretical and static; both are meant to be
experiential and on-going. Both are for growing, intimate,
fulfilling *communion.*

Union without communion is contact, not relationship.
Any marriage that includes union without communion—
two-way communication and intimacy—is not a true
marriage. In the same way, our spiritual union with Christ
is not complete and will bear little fruit unless there is a
two-way communication and intimacy on the spirit level.
Our one-sided praying—the endless monologues most of
us engage in—needs to be enlarged to include some form
of interior or contemplative prayer which allows for
listening. In centering prayer we stop our monologue and
take time to be still and listen to God at the inner level of
our being.

Most of us have known little about life-giving spiritual
communion with Christ, our heavenly Spouse. Our
spiritual marriages are shallow and barren. No wonder
the Christian life has not even come close to living up to
our expectations. No wonder the measure of love, joy,
peace, and fulfillment we so ardently anticipated has so
consistently eluded us.

What's been wrong? Why hasn't our marriage to Christ

worked? When will the fruit of our spiritual marriage finally be evident to all?

As I said in the previous chapter, my answer to these questions is found in the single, simple faith-practice of contemplation, or centering—of learning to be still and "be" to God. We have all been taught endlessly to do, do, do. But who has ever taught us to be, be, be?

Contemplation is not merely thinking about God so as to know Him better; it is stopping and allowing ourselves to *be known by Him*. In the first experience, which I would call *meditation*, we are the initiators—our reasoning, our concepts, and our words are the medium to accomplish our goals. In true *contemplation*, on the other hand, we recognize God as the Initiator—and our only purpose is to give our total attention to His presence in us.

Though the injunction to "meditate" on God's Law and precepts is given nine times in Psalms, the specific words "contemplate" and "contemplation" are never used anywhere in Scripture. There are passages, however, that describe the faith-practice of contemplative prayer. Two verses have been especially important for me.

The first is II Corinthians 3:18—"But we all, with unveiled face beholding as in a mirror the glory of the Lord, are being transformed into the same image from glory to glory...." This is God's clear promise of transformation to all who behold (contemplate) the immanent Christ, as well as adore the transcendent Lord. Our destiny is to be divinized—to be hid in Christ, to be incorporated into the Trinity. But that metamorphosis takes place only as we behold Christ and allow His glory in us to be reflected to our world. To use a metaphor, we are moons that reflect the Sun's light and glory; we would never presume to become the Sun. God is always the Source, the Initiator; we are always the responders, the reactors, the reflectors.

A key phrase in this verse on contemplation is "unveiled

face." We see the significance of these words two verses earlier where we read: "But whenever a person turns to the Lord the veil is taken away" (v. 16). It's when we turn within to the Lord and behold His Presence as in a mirror, that the veil—the veil of separation and blindness—is removed, thereby freeing the Spirit to do His transforming work.

For me, the second most important verse on contemplative prayer is Romans 8:26. "We do not know how to pray worthily as sons of God, but His Spirit within us is actually praying for us in those agonizing longings which never find words" (J. B. Phillip's *New Testament in Modern English*). When all of our concepts and imaginings and words come to an end, and we are down to our longings and groanings, the Holy Spirit takes over. In effect, we are saying, "Holy Spirit, pray for me. I have nothing more to say." It's at that point that the faithful Spirit within us prays—not only on our behalf, but in our place—for ourselves, for others, for the world and for all that God desires.

It seems clear that this is a level of interior prayer that goes far deeper than the verbalized acknowledgments, praise and petitions that most of us practice. Let's face it—there is a vast difference between all the meditative prayer words, thoughts, reasonings and images that we conjure up and the silent, heart-centered, contemplative prayer which flows from the depths of our being. While it is all truly prayer, we tend to choose the first part and leave the latter part undone.

4

BASKING IN
HIS PRESENCE

The salient aspect of the spiritual life is a given one: union with God. We are endowed with Spirit from on high. There is no way that we can become identical with God. But we can become deified.

We do not become totally human until we become partly divine. God became man, as St. Athanasius said, so that man might become God. It is God (who is love, and love is diffusive) who takes the initiative, unites Himself to us, keeps us alive by His creative and attentive presence, and with no violence, but with the gentle fury of an irrepressible and invincible love, touches us where we are most free and invites us, seductively, into the intimate and infinite love-life of the Trinity.

What we need to do is sensitively recognize who we are—brides of the Bridegroom (that is why Greek, Latin, and Spanish all use feminine words for soul: *psyche, anima, alma*)—and be aware of what is going on: we are being led to the bridal chamber.

In other words, realization of the union with God we already enjoy, responding in every way we know how to the overture of God's love, adoringly recognizing His presence in a broken but marvelously transparent world—that's what the spiritual life is all about.

—*William McNamara*

4

BASKING IN
HIS PRESENCE

The visit of Jesus to the home of Mary and Martha of Bethany is a familiar story to all of us. It is also the classic illustration of the distinction between contemplation and busyness, between being and doing. And it is because that image of Mary sitting in silence at the feet of Jesus so beautifully captures the faith-practice of "basking in His presence" that I chose it for the cover picture of this book. No other image comes to my mind more often during my personal times of contemplative prayer.

You remember the story. As Martha is busy in the kitchen preparing food for her special Guest, she glances into the living room. There is Jesus, just sitting, with Mary lounging at His feet. Mary is saying nothing, content just to enjoy Jesus' presence and to listen intently when He says something.

More tasks in the kitchen, and a few more glances into the living room, are more than Martha can handle. Hands on hips, she strides to the doorway and announces, "Lord, don't You care that my sister has left me to do all the work by myself? Tell her to help me!"

Martha's problem wasn't her doing, her good work ethic; that was commendable. The problem was that she didn't know how to "be." This was revealed in the way she judged her unnamed "sister."

Jesus slowly looks up only long enough to challenge Martha with these words: "Martha, Martha, you are worried and bothered about so many things; but only a few things are necessary, really only one: for Mary has chosen the good part, which shall not be taken away from her" (Luke 10:41-42).

The commentators can argue all they want about the various meanings of the "one thing necessary" and "the good part," but virtually all of them agree that Jesus clearly commends Mary's priorities. One translator (Beck) uses these words, "Mary has made the right choice." One thing is sure: we cannot let our "doing" replace our "being," for service that does not flow out of relationship and love is worthless. It's not a question of either/or, it's a question of priority.

For me, the "one thing necessary," now that I have found the pearl of great price, is being attentive to God—it's basking in His presence, it's "hanging out" with my Friend, it's looking into the eyes of my Lover, it's communing in the secret place at the ground of my being, it's wanting to be lost in my oneness with Him. The "one thing necessary" can be expressed in many other ways, but the fact is that we must learn to "be." We are humans *beings,* not human "thinkings," or human "doings."

But how do we learn to be? How do we learn to rest? How can experiential union become a reality for us? Granted, we are all on a lifelong journey of faith, but how and when will we accept the gift of experiential union that goes beyond all the theory, words and self-effort?

The Christian mystics through the centuries have all shared the same answer to the foregoing questions. Though they might have called it by different names, they have all recommended the same faith-practice of contemplative prayer, a prayer of adoration.

In recent years, a few monastics have led the way in bringing lay-people in both Roman Catholic and Protestant circles to an awareness of the simplicity and fruitfulness of contemplative, or "centering," prayer. My mentors have been three Cistercians (a monastic order founded in the eleventh century): Thomas Merton, Thomas Keating and M. Basil Pennington. Centering prayer is summarized by Pennington in his book, *Centering Prayer*, as follows:

1. *Sit relaxed and quiet.*
2. *Be in faith and love to God who dwells in the center of your being.*
3. *Take up a love word and let it be gently present, supporting your being to God in faith-filled love.*
4. *Whenever you become aware of anything else, simply, gently return to the Lord with the use of your prayer word.*
5. *Close by letting the "Our Father" (or some other familiar prayer) pray itself through you.*

Seems simple enough. All we have to do is "be still" and consent to His presence within. We focus our minds on nothing but His presence. As we do this in faith twice a day, for from five to twenty minutes each time, we will be engaging in the prayer of silence, as taught by the Desert Fathers and others for centuries.

Yes, it seems simple, but you will be amazed at how difficult it is. You will be surprised and dismayed at how short your attention span is. You will be plagued by thoughts about everything under the sun. You will be tempted to judge your "performance." This temptation needs to be resisted. God judges only our heart intent, and so should we. And our basic heart intent, when we choose contemplation, is to seek God for Himself.

The use of a "love word," recommended not only by Pennington but by most writers on contemplative prayer, turns out to be quite helpful and necessary. Let God lead you to a short word that captures for you the focus, the intention and the attentiveness of your mind and heart to God's presence within you. Whenever your mind wanders and you become aware of your thoughts, simply use your love word to return to an awareness of His presence.

In time, the use of the prayer word becomes so natural that it is more of a sigh than a pronounced word. Pennington explains: "It is not an effortful proclamation or a constantly repeated mantra, but rather an occasional sigh of love, a murmur of love, a being to."

Some of the prayer words suggested by various writers and my personal friends include: Abba, Father, home, Jesus, peace, rest, yes. I currently use the word "bask."

Thomas Keating suggests that instead of, or in addition to, a "sacred word," you may be led to use a "sacred glance." You may find that a simple image will best bring you back to an awareness of God's presence. For me, the recurrent image of Mary sitting at the feet of Jesus has been most effective in helping me refocus. Marge has found that the image that comes to her during her times of being still is that of the little children coming to Jesus. She sees herself as one of those children.

The choice of a "love-word," or "sacred gaze," as well as other techniques used in centering prayer, are matters between you and your Lover. The Scripture gives no detailed instructions, only general guidelines: "Come to Me," "Wait on the Lord," and "Beholding as in a mirror the glory of the Lord."

Certain words are probably best avoided as prayer words. At one of our Glen Ellyn conferences, after we had suggested some possibilities, a friend who knew me pretty well lightened up our session when he interjected, "I think Bill would do better in his centering if he stopped using 'Dow Jones' as his prayer word." (Obviously, this is not my prayer word, but my friend was more right than he knew, as thoughts about the stock market are frequently a major distraction for me!)

Techniques recommended by writers on contemplative prayer are as varied as those used in other types of prayer and meditative practices. Some suggest a focus on one's breathing, instead of the use of a prayer word. Others recommend using a mantra—a constantly repeated word or phrase.

For example, the late John Main of Canada was adamant that the word *Maranatha* (the greeting used by the first century Church, meaning "the Lord cometh") be repeated slowly in time with one's breathing. Inhaling, one slowly and quietly says "mara-"; exhaling, one says "-natha." Others recommend the repeated use of the Jesus Prayer ("Lord Jesus Christ, Son of the living God, have mercy on me, a sinner"), or some other short, meaningful phrase.

I prefer not to evaluate any of the endless suggestions and recommendations of whether to use a "love word" or a mantra; of how long, how often, where or when to have a centering time; or of what meditative practices should be used prior to and after one's centering time. I say with Paul, "Let each one be fully persuaded in his own mind."

My present practice is to spend much more time in active worship—which includes all my church attendance and activities, my participation in seminars and retreats, my devotional readings, as well as everything I've been doing for years in my "quiet times"—than I spend in actual centering, or contemplation.

But I am convinced that the few minutes I spend each day in contemplative prayer are more life-changing than all my other spiritual practices combined. James Finley, in his book, *Merton's Palace of Nowhere*, doesn't hedge about the value of contemplative prayer when he writes: "In fidelity to silent prayer there is unveiled the possibility of infinite growth in union with God."

Whether we go to church or some other get-together, read a spiritual book, study or memorize the Bible, pray the Scriptures, engage in intercessory prayer, or write in our journal, all these worthy practices should be preliminary to the main event: the few minutes during which we behold our Lover within, in solitude and silence.

5

FROM COMPULSIVENESS TO CONTENTMENT

In the eternal plan of God, Christ has the central position. Because of His infinite power, the Eternal Word has taken the entire human family into a divine relationship with the Father.

We who are incomplete, confused and riddled with the consequences of original sin constitute the human family that the Son of God took upon Himself. The basic thrust of Jesus' message is to invite us into divine union, which is the sole remedy for the human predicament.

Lacking the experience of divine union, we feel alienated from ourselves, God, other people and the cosmos. Hence, we seek substitutes for the happiness for which we are predestined, but which we do not know how to find. This misguided search for happiness is the human predicament that the Gospel addresses.

Happiness can only be found in the experience of union with God, the experience that also unites us to everyone else in the human family and to all reality. This return to unity is the good news that Jesus proclaimed.

—*Thomas Keating*

5

FROM COMPULSIVENESS TO CONTENTMENT

Our destiny in Christ is to be changed from glory to glory, until we have grown up in all aspects of Him who is our Head, even Christ. Our destiny is fulfilled only to the extent that we respond to the Lord's call to live in the inner reality of our *true self* in Christ, instead of in the outer, illusory reality of the separated *false self*.

Freedom and wholeness surface gradually, in proportion to our seeing things as they really are—that is, from God's eternal viewpoint. But the process of becoming a whole person is impeded by our ignorance of just how much the false self continues to govern our lives. Even if we are aware of some of our obvious weaknesses of the flesh, most of us are blind to the hidden flaws that cause us to continue to live fragmented and dysfunctional lives. Our false selves are insidious and unrelenting masters, taking an incredible toll on each of us.

We have all grown up wounded, to some extent, because our parents and other role-models were partially dysfunctional. They could not teach us what they did not know. So it's not surprising that we assimilated many of the false programs for happiness which they taught us by word and example. Our parents initiated us into the false-self lifestyle, and it was further drilled into us by other family members, our peers, books, movies and TV. Directly or indirectly, from our very first breath we have all been subject to an overwhelming dose of distorted, selfish human values.

So it is also not surprising that from our earliest days we have gradually become craving, clinging, controlling creatures. This is false self: compulsiveness in every shape and form. We see it in toddlers, in grade-schoolers, in teens, in young marrieds, in adults, and in seniors—no one is immune. And sad to say, in most people the compulsiveness only gets worse with age.

To my knowledge, no writer in our generation has spelled out the problem of false self and its only solution more clearly than Thomas Keating. His trilogy (*Open Mind, Open Heart; The Mystery of Christ;* and *Invitation to Love*) elucidates all aspects of our universal, lifelong spiritual journey from false self to true self.

The false self, we are told, is motivated by its "instinctive needs for survival and security, for affection and esteem, and for power and control over as much of life as possible." Keating first traces the psychological roots and development of the false self from birth to physical maturity. No one, he suggests, is immune to the various false programs for happiness that the world foists upon us. Next he introduces us to the potential of the true self brought about by our transforming union with God and our awareness of the indwelling Christ.

True maturity comes only when we let go of the compulsions and addictions which false self has fomented in our lives. We need to be liberated, to arrive at a contentment which comes only from detachment. We need to experience a release from our craving, clinging, controlling compulsiveness. We need to move ever more from self-centered false self to Christ-centered true self.

Being a pragmatic lawyer, CPA and a businessman,

with no formal training in psychology, philosophy or religion, I needed to simplify and distill Keating's teachings for my own use. To help me to understand and remember who I am and who I am not, I've summarized the problem of false self in a three-letter acronym: SEC. No, not the Securities and Exchange Commission, but *security*, *esteem* and *control*.

Our upbringing, culture and environment have conditioned most of us to believe that we would be happier if only we could have more security, more esteem and more control. In other words, we are convinced that if we had more things, were loved and understood, and had more power and control over our world, it would change everything. We mistakenly assume that SEC is the formula for happiness. Madison Avenue has brainwashed Americans into believing that happiness comes to those who look to creatures and created things for their contentment and personal fulfillment. But the media is wrong. The self-centered value system of "I, Me, My, Mine" doesn't bring fulfillment. This formula brings chaos, not contentment.

The more compulsively we crave *security*—financially, as well as in health and in relationships—the more elusive our goal of security becomes.

The first priority in life for many of us is to earn enough money to comfortably live the "American dream." Our second priority is trying to amass enough wealth to be able to live comfortably in our golden years. Recently, I read an article by a financial expert who warned that, because of inflation, those retiring after the year 2020 should plan to have an estate of at least one and a half million dollars if they hope to maintain their standard of living. The problem is that even most two-income families have to go into debt in order to meet their current "needs." So adequate financial security for retirement has become an impossible moving target for most people.

Security in the area of personal health—as well as in the health of family and friends—is equally elusive. Health is here today and gone tomorrow. In spite of rigorous exercise programs, vitamins, food supplements, endless diets and the best doctors and medicines money can buy, health addicts and body-fussers of every ilk are still devastated by disease, injury and premature death.

And achieving security in family relationships is also an impossible dream. Over half of all marriages in the United States end in divorce, and all too few of the other half are happy and fulfilling. We raise our children with high hopes, only to find that the various internal pressures in the family unit make unconditional acceptance among family members a virtual impossibility. Many of our dreams for our extended families and friends turn into nightmares. Only as we mature do we come to realize that no one but God is capable of unconditional acceptance, day after day, year after year.

The second instinct of false self is to search for *esteem*. In due course we all find that our attempts to find happiness through the esteem of others is both frustrating and inadequate. At home and at the work place—where most adults spend the better part of their lives—we end up experiencing disillusionment. Hard as we try to gain the esteem, respect, acceptance, admiration and love of those around us, we can never quite please everyone.

My teenage grandchildren have given me a new insight into the problem of self-esteem, as well as a new appreciation of the word "cool." Whether they are talking about buying a CD, new clothes, a pair of athletic shoes, their first car, or whatever, there is only one ultimately determining question: is it "cool"? In other words, what will my peers think? Will my choice impress them and gain their approval and esteem? Any rational discussion of comparative price and value, cost of maintenance, parental opinion, decency, or anything else, is irrelevant because, to them, there is only one litmus test: "Will my friends think it's cool?" If they don't, save your breath; they wouldn't buy it, wear it, or use it on a bet. They might not recognize this, but they have been taken in by the second false program for happiness: being esteemed by others. And it's not just teenagers who need to be "cool." All too many of us make our decisions based on what others think. We let everyone "pull our strings."

The third manifestation of false self is our passion for *control*. The compulsion to control, to be in charge, to make everything predictable and in line with our desires and convictions is manifest wherever you look. When was the last time you had a conversation in which you completed your point without being interrupted at least once? And, by the same token, how easily do you give up control of the conversation and allow others to speak? Of course, it's hard to listen to others when we have all the answers and see ourselves as experts on everything.

Marge and I attend a Sunday School class which consists mainly of middle-aged, professional adults. Every quarter we choose a different "spiritual" book to read and use as the basis of our class discussions. A different person leads our discussion each Sunday. The big joke in the class is how often the issue of "control" comes up. The propensity to want to control seems to be a factor in every discussion on the Christian life. And, it seems that everyone in the class is acutely aware of the fact that we are all prone to be know-it-all's—at home, at work, with friends, as well as in our class. So, whenever "control" is mentioned, a chorus of self-conscious, knowing laughs sweeps over our whole class.

What's the alternative to the world's programs for happiness? If SEC—security, esteem and control—doesn't work, what does?

When Jesus began His public ministry, He immediately pointed the multitudes to the true keys to happiness. In the eight "Be-attitudes" with which He began the Sermon on the Mount, Jesus proposed a program for happiness that was radically different from that which most of us have been taught in the past.

The Beatitudes are a summary of life lived free of false self. Jesus said that happiness (blessedness) comes to those who are poor in spirit, to those who mourn, to those who are gentle, to those who hunger and thirst after righteousness, to those who are merciful, to those who are peacemakers, and to those who are persecuted for righteousness. Jesus affirmed life lived from the inside out—looking to the Christ within, looking to God alone, as the only way to fulfillment.

Christ calls us to give up our useless pursuit of creatures and things. The endless list of attachments demanded by false self is to be replaced by detachment from all these things. Only through consciousness of our love-union in Christ will we see things the way they really are.

St. Augustine was right when he said, "For Yourself You have made us, O, God, and our heart is restless until it rests in You." Our Beloved, God alone, is meant to be our sole source of fulfillment and happiness.

Liberation comes only when we live as we were created to live—when instead of trying to guarantee our happiness based on SEC, we move from compulsiveness to contentment, when we respond to His call to lay our burdens down and come to Him and "find rest."

6

THE RESIDENT PSYCHOTHERAPIST

Through Jesus, I see a God who offers to baptize, marry, heal, and transform the ego. Whether our most deeply-rooted problem is caused by sin or by wound, or (most likely) by a combination of the two, through Jesus we see a God who with inexorable power of compassion calls forth the innermost, most hidden self of shame, weakness, and hurt into a healed life.

No matter how distorted and hurtful our powers within, they were originally created from the divine source, and they hold the potentiality for the unique and the beautiful. In their healing, they are not wiped out or destroyed, for nothing in God's creation can ultimately be destroyed. Rather, they are restored to their original, intended power of gifted creativity.

Our fear, when healed, becomes intuitive, empathic compassion and sensitivity towards others. Our destructive anger, when healed, becomes a passion, a hunger and thirst for justice and righteousness. Our perfectionism, our compulsion to organize and dominate, when healed, becomes released, joyous power to build and create. Our inertia and withdrawals, when healed, become increasing powers for peace and integrity. Our possessiveness, our jealousies, and our physical addictions, when healed, become growing released powers to become lovers and healers to the world around us.

—Flora Slosson Wuellner

6

THE RESIDENT PSYCHOTHERAPIST

One of my joys as a grandfather is to tell stories to my younger grandchildren. Fairly regularly they demand, almost in a chorus: "Papa, tell us a story!"

"Well, what story would you like this time?" I ask.

They often have an old favorite in mind, and will ask me to repeat a story from my childhood, or from World War II, or from my various near-death experiences.

At other times they say, "Tell us a Jesus story." And the Jesus story they most frequently ask for is "the story about how Jesus healed the lady who was bleeding." They can never quite remember the word "hemorrhage." (And I can never quite remember how to spell it!)

I never tire of telling it, as it has all the ingredients of a great story: a poor woman who has been abused by her doctors and now needs special help, and a story-book hero who miraculously and lovingly meets her needs.

After hemorrhaging for twelve years and spending all her money on many doctors, this woman heard that the healer, Jesus, was in town. She slipped up behind Him, touched the fringe of His cloak, and was instantly healed.

Jesus, as you remember, wheeled around and said, "Who touched Me?"

The disciples all quickly made a disclaimer, with Peter

saying, in effect, "What do You mean, 'Who touched Me?' Hundreds of people are pressing all around us and You say, 'Who touched Me!' Who knows?" But Jesus knew, for power had gone out of Him—someone had touched Him in faith.

It's at this point in the story that I really get dramatic. I get down on my knees, pretend I'm looking up at Jesus, and say to the grandchildren, "So the woman knelt in front of Jesus and said, 'Lord, it was I. I needed to be healed, so I touched You—and I was healed!'"

Then I close with my favorite line: "Then, with love in His eyes and in His voice, Jesus said, 'Yes, I knew it was you, My daughter. It's O.K. Your faith has made you whole. Go in peace!'"

In recent years this demonstration of Jesus' healing power has taken on a new meaning for me, so that I see it as far more than a simple physical healing. It now means that if only I will reach out and touch Him at the center of my being in my times of contemplative prayer, His power can also heal and transform me from within.

The world has a whole range of solutions to help people handle their psychotic and neurotic thoughts and behavior. These include encounter groups, support groups, 12-step programs, private counselling and psychotherapy, as well as more extreme solutions, like hypnosis and even exorcism. The problem with all these solutions is that to some extent they involve the reliving of the traumatic experiences that caused our dysfunctionality in the first place. I was personally reluctant to go through all that trauma. Wasn't there some way to free my mind without dredging up all my traumatic experiences and refocusing on them?

As I mentioned in Chapter One, this question was answered for me by a single, simple sentence in Thomas Keating's *Open Mind, Open Heart.* "If you are faithful to the daily practice of contemplative prayer, your psychic wounds will be healed without your being re-traumatized." Ever since reading that sentence, I have looked to the Christ who I know lives within me as my Resident Psychotherapist. Every day, usually twice a day, I come "home" to practice His presence, to wait upon Him in silence—even if just for a few minutes.

When I first started centering, I used the word "heal" as my prayer word, because I was very conscious of my need to be healed of my obvious dysfunctionality. At each centering time, I visualized myself as coming to Christ to touch the hem of His garment for inner healing.

Later, because throughout my life I have always found it easier to *do* than *be,* I changed my prayer word to "rest," as I felt I needed to "let go and let God." Then for a time I used the word "yes," as it seemed to capture in just three letters the basic intention of my heart, as well as the spirit of two significant phrases in the Lord's prayer, "Thy kingdom come, Thy will be done." If you were down to one word in your vocabulary, what word could be more pleasing to God than "yes, yes, yes"?

Then, after about a year of "centering," the Lord led me to my current prayer word, "bask." Most of my life I have been a compulsive, helter-skelter doer—and always in a hurry. I had never taken much time to bask in anyone or anything. I needed to learn to ask less and to bask more. I needed to wrestle less and nestle more; to struggle less and snuggle more.

So at this time I usually use the word "bask" in my times of centering, though I occasionally still use the word "heal." These are the two words that remind me most of the two reasons I silently "practice His presence": to joyfully bask in the presence of my indwelling Lover, and to anticipate the healing power and transformation that flows to anyone who reaches out in faith to touch Jesus.

There are two verses in Scripture that specifically

mention transformation. One calls us to "be transformed," while the other says that we "are being transformed."

The first is Romans 12:2: "And do not be conformed to this world, but be transformed by the renewing of your mind...." This is a well-known and much-quoted verse, but what is Paul really speaking about when he says that we should be transformed by the renewing of the mind? I'm convinced that the day-to-day renewing of the mind refers to the necessary therapy of the psyche, and that this is best handled by our Resident Psychotherapist, Christ Himself. All we can do is open ourselves by faith to "be transformed" by Him. We don't transform ourselves; we trust God to bring it about as a gift.

The second "transformation" verse is one that we looked at earlier. It's II Corinthians 3:18—"But we all, with unveiled face beholding as in a mirror the glory of the Lord, are being transformed into the same image from glory to glory...." Even as I was typing this verse, I looked up at my family-room wall and re-read the following Juan Carlos Ortiz quotation on a plaque I received as a gift:

> *Look at yourself in a mirror ...*
> *You are an expression of the glorified*
> *eternal Christ who lives within you.*
> *Begin to believe that about yourself*
> *and you will start to experience*
> *His life as a daily reality.*

We will not experience His life as a daily reality, or believe we are precious persons, until we begin to see ourselves as unique expressions of the Christ who lives within us. As one song writer puts it: "You who are God's great treasure, He finds His pleasure in you." Yes, we are His treasure, and we do give Him pleasure. And be clear about this: you are precious!

Beholding Christ within by faith will result in our being transformed into the image and likeness of Christ. It will also change our perception of ourselves. Though we must refrain from being scorekeepers who look for preconceived feelings or manifestations, Juan Carlos Ortiz is right: we will start to experience Christ's life as a daily reality only when we begin to believe that we are expressions of the Christ who lives within us and that nothing can separate us from Him.

Most books and articles on contemplative prayer emphasize that our focus should be on Christ—on a giving of ourselves to our Lover—not a focus on self and what we can get out of it. However, I must confess that for the first couple of years of my centering practice, my perceived need was so great that my priority was just to touch the hem of His garment for inner healing. Being with Him for Himself, or giving myself to Him in love, were almost incomprehensible to me at the time.

In the months and years that have passed since I first started reading about contemplative prayer, I have continued to read one book after another. Interestingly, 90% of what I read is by Roman Catholic writers— monks, priests, professors and lay people who have practiced solitude, silence and contemplative prayer for years, and have experienced its life-transforming power. Carlo Caretto, James Finley, William Johnston, Thomas Merton, Henri Nouwen, M. Basil Pennington, William Shannon, and Thomas Keating are eight of the authors who have guided me over the past six years with their writings. But I haven't just *read about* centering prayer—I have consistently practiced the prayer of silence.

The prayer of the mouth must give way to the prayer of the heart. The word uttered by our lips must give way to the Living Word within us. Our outer prayer of beseeching, reasoning, seeking and doing must be aided by our inner, contemplative prayer of surrender, intuition, receiving and being.

It's only when we become poor in spirit—when we realize our bankruptcy, when we are convinced that we do not know how to pray—that wordless, Word-filled prayer takes over. Is it incongruous to use both adjectives—"wordless" and "Word-filled"—for the prayer of silence? No, for it is when the words of our mouths and minds finally cease that the inner Living Word fills the silence.

Though the wording of Romans 8:26, 27 in the Concordant Literal New Testament is a bit awkward, when read carefully it seems to me to be wonderfully clear and accurate—

> *Now, similarly, the Spirit also is aiding our infirmity, for what we should be praying for, in accord with what must be, we are not aware, but the Spirit itself is pleading for us with inarticulate groanings.*

"For what we should be praying for, we are not aware." Might this not mean that the Spirit pleads to the Father on our behalf only when we come to the end of our self-effort—to the end of all our words, concepts and agendas?

Through the years I had always practiced *verbalized prayer*—prayer with words. Since the days of my Charismatic experience I had rarely missed an extended night or early morning session of talking with God. These sessions were wonderful, spiritually beneficial times. But they weren't true conversations; they were monologues. I did all the talking; my mind and my mouth never stopped. I never listened. God couldn't get a word in edgewise even if He tried.

My faith-practice of *contemplative prayer*—prayer without words—opened a new and wonderful (wonder-filled) world for me. No longer did I have to figure out what to pray for, or lay out in detail for God His various options. Now I could just "be still and know" that He is God. I learned, in faith, to simply wait on God in silence, with the sole intention of being with Him, my indwelling Lover.

This promise of Scripture is clear: "Those that wait on the Lord will not be disappointed." And I haven't been disappointed. A large measure of love, joy and peace—along with the other fruits of the Spirit—has become a reality for me. How wonderful it is to not feel self-conscious and embarrassed when I tell people that I love them, to be able to smile again as I did as a youth, and to have inner peace when the tensions of life threaten to swamp me.

When I was first led to start a magazine emphasizing the believer's union with Christ, the Lord clearly gave me its name: *Union Life*. I knew it had to say "Union," but "Life"? It has taken me a few years, but now I understand the title's full significance. Union must be more than just a naked concept, more than a theological position, more than simply "knowing-about." Union is meant to be experiential; it is for communion with God; it is for *life*—a life-transforming love affair with the Lover within.

I am personally convinced that it is in response to my daily practice of wordless prayer—"beholding as in a mirror the glory of the Lord"—that my Resident Psychotherapist has begun a healing of my deep-seated dysfunctionality. Because of that healing, I am beginning to know abundant *life* as Jesus said His followers would: "I am come that you might have life...abundantly." And I believe that healing and transformation and abundant life is available to all who come home to Him in solitude and silence.

7

UNCONDITIONAL
LOVE

In the Gospel of Luke we read: "Peter said, 'Man, I do not know what you are talking about.' At that moment, while he was yet speaking, a cock crew; and the Lord turned and looked straight at Peter...and Peter went outside and wept bitterly."

I had a fairly good relationship with the Lord. I would ask Him for things, converse with Him, praise Him, thank Him.

But always I had this uncomfortable feeling that He wanted me to look at Him, and I would not. I would talk, but look away when I sensed He was looking at me.

I was afraid. I was afraid that I might find an accusation there of some unrepented sin. I thought I might find a demand there; there would be something He wanted from me.

One day I finally summoned up courage and looked! There was no accusation. There was no demand. The eyes just said, "I love you."

And I walked out and, like Peter, I wept.

—*Anthony de Mello*

7

UNCONDITIONAL LOVE

Our Sunday School class recently read one of Paul Tillich's books, *The Courage to Be*. Though much of Tillich's complex thinking and terminology went way over my head, he said one thing in the last chapter which made the book more than worthwhile for me. It's a quote I never want to forget: "Life is accepting His acceptance."

"Accepting His acceptance"—what a profound statement! But how does one do it?

God's unconditional love and acceptance of us is certainly a major ingredient of the "good news" we have all been straining to hear all of our lives. But, in my case, no truth has been more elusive than that of His total acceptance, unconditional love and great delight in me. Though I've never had any doubts about His basic love for me as demonstrated in Jesus, or in my eternal salvation since my conversion at the age of eight, accepting His "unconditional love" has been another matter.

My entire background, as well as my personality, had set me up to accept and reject myself and others totally on the basis of performance. My parents were typical "Protestant work-ethic" Germans. My four years in Naval Aviation in World War II reinforced "performance" as the basis for accepting or rejecting others. The business world in which I practiced as an accountant/lawyer for years taught me the same outlook: life is serious business and everything is based on results. That's the "bottom line." Despite the best intentions of all those involved in my Christian upbringing, including those in my church, I didn't know what "pure grace" meant. I still assumed that some measure of performance was a prerequisite to God's total acceptance and unconditional love.

Therefore, being unable to reach the high standards I had set for myself, I never saw myself as totally acceptable. As a result, I had a poor self-image for most of my life. As I saw it, I never quite measured up to what I thought was demanded of me—by God, by my family, by my associates, and certainly by myself. The resulting lack of genuine self-esteem made it impossible for me to function as a whole person in my relationship with God or with others. How could I love God, or love and affirm the people around me, when I did not love myself? But God was not finished with me yet.

In 1989 I went to the Chicago production of *Les Miserables*. First performed in London in 1985, *Les Miz*, as it is affectionately known by many, has been seen by more people than any other play ever produced. I sat through the performance virtually entranced, and before the last curtain fell, I had two new heroes: the Bishop and Jean Valjean. Their gentleness and acts of compassion had captured my heart.

Heroes are special gifts from God who inspire us to dream impossible dreams and to see through our outer limitations to new vistas within. As a kid, my heroes included Abe Lincoln and several sports figures. As a Christian adult, I was inspired by certain religious leaders and devout people of faith. Although my two new heroes did not fit the typical hero mold, it was through them that God would teach me something of the glory of unconditional love.

In the following months, I watched both the 1935 movie and the 1981 technicolor film of *Les Miserables*. I read the complete 1400-page novel, as well as two different abridged versions. Whenever I was driving, alone or with the family, I listened endlessly to the penetrating musical score of the Cameron Mackintosh production. In the next few years I went to the play twelve more times in five different cities. I'm not sure exactly what it was that so obsessively attracted me to *Les Miz*. I suppose it was the wonderful crimson thread of redemption, forgiveness and unconditional love which is woven throughout the story of Jean Valjean—just as it is throughout Scripture.

Based on Victor Hugo's classic French novel of 1862, *Les Miz* (the musical) is a moving account of an ex-convict, Jean Valjean, whose life is miraculously transformed by a one-night encounter with an elderly bishop.

Jean Valjean, as a young man, goes to prison for five years for stealing a loaf of bread for his widowed sister and her starving children. He makes four attempts to escape, and each time his jail sentence is increased.

After being treated like an animal for twenty years, a bitter, cynical Valjean is finally released. A few days later, he has a life-changing experience when he meets the Bishop, who treats him with love and understanding. In faith, the Bishop "buys" Valjean's soul with two silver candlesticks and some other silver pieces which Valjean had stolen from him. It wasn't theological words or arguments that broke Valjean's hardened heart; it was the Bishop's forgiveness, acceptance and unconditional love.

Valjean changes his name and his ways, and becomes a prosperous businessman. He lives confidently and compassionately, never forgetting the night he experienced the grace of God and the unconditional love of the Bishop.

But events eventually transpire in such a way that

Valjean must either expose himself as an ex-convict who broke his parole, or see an innocent man imprisoned in his place. He is confronted with an awful dilemma: to admit to his true identity and go back to prison, or to spend the rest of his life living a lie.

In "Who am I?", my favorite song in the play, Jean Valjean sings: "If I speak, I am condemned; if I stay silent, I am damned." So he asks himself the question we all should ask when we are confronted with temptation: "Who am I?"

After much soul searching, he screams out, "I'm Jean Valjean! 24601 [his prison number]!" He cries, "My soul belongs to God, I know; I made that bargain long ago." He knows he is a transformed Jean Valjean. He might look the same, but he is completely changed. He knows he is not his own; he has been bought with a price.

When we see ourselves as new creations in Christ, hard decisions become easier—in one sense we no longer have a "choice." We must be true to our real selves. We must choose the way of unconditional love, the way of righteousness, irrespective of the personal cost.

Above all, we must be absolutely aware of who we really are. Remember, we are not human beings having random spiritual experiences; we are spiritual beings having human experiences. The Scripture says, "He who has joined himself to Christ is one spirit with Him." We are not independent beings separated from God—we are human expressions of the Divine Lover with whom we are one. Self-centered choices are replaced with love choices. The Lover now lives within us.

The first chapter of the *Les Miserables* novel is entitled, "An Upright Man." Victor Hugo introduces his readers to the 76-year old Bishop by recounting several episodes that show why everyone in the small French village so love and respect this extraordinary man. He then summarizes the Bishop's everyday life as follows:

> *The Bishop's day was full to the brim with good*
> *thoughts, good words, and good actions. Still the day*
> *was not complete if cold or wet weather prevented him*
> *from spending an hour or two in the garden before*
> *going to bed.... He was alone with himself, collected,*
> *peaceful, adoring, comparing the serenity of his heart*
> *with that of the Other, affected in the darkness by the*
> *visible splendor of the constellations, and the invisible*
> *splendor of God.... He dreamed of the grandeur and*
> *presence of God.... Without seeking to comprehend the*
> *incomprehensible, he gazed at it. He did not study*
> *God: he was dazzled by Him.*

Evidently the Bishop's faith-practice of silent contemplation, in addition to his consistent mental meditation, had transformed him into a man of humility, gentleness, compassion and, above all, unconditional love. No wonder the Bishop continues to be a hero for me. I, too, want to be so dazzled by God's inner presence that the transcendent transformation experienced by the Bishop will bit by bit become my everyday experience.

Although I don't have a garden to walk in as the Bishop did, I do have a large deck outside my second-story apartment that overlooks a 30-acre park. So, following the lead of my hero, the Bishop, I frequently spend time in the late hours of the evening or early hours of the morning in meditation and contemplation, being dazzled by both the visible splendor of the stars and the invisible splendor of the Bright and Morning Star within.

Some time before my introduction to *Les Miserables*, in separate encounters with two of my children, I was faced with a surprising truth about myself.

My only son, Scott, has been my best male friend for many years. Working with Scott at my motel, and in our coin shop during the eighties, we spent most of every day together. We came to rely on each other and know each other quite intimately. One day I had casually made a comment like, "You know, Scott, I'm not always going to be around."

At which point Scott interrupted me and said vehemently, "Don't talk like that, Dad. You can't die! I hope I die before you. I can't imagine life without you!"

I left it at that, but Scott's adamant statement caused me to ponder. *Why would Scott react so passionately at the thought of my not being around any more? Was anyone that important to me?*

Some time later I had a comparable conversation with my youngest daughter, Valerie. Again, I made an offhand remark about dying. Valerie was aghast. She said something like, "You're not going to die, Dad! You can't. I can't even think of living without you around. Don't say another word about it!" End of conversation. Her abrupt reaction, much like Scott's, brought his words back to my mind. I said to myself: *What's going on here? Why are these kids responding like this?*

Such emotion was incomprehensible to me. And, after thinking about it for a while, I had to admit to myself that I didn't feel that way about anyone.

Both of the foregoing encounters came to my mind the first time I saw *Les Miz*. The death scene at the end contains words that have an uncanny parallel to what Scott and Valerie said to me.

Jean Valjean and his daughter, Cosette, had been separated for a few months, and both had wondered if they would ever see each other again. As it turns out, a reunion does take place in Valjean's apartment. After some preliminaries, and after Valjean thanks God for allowing him to see Cosette and her husband Marius once again, Valjean announces; "I shall die in a few minutes."

In one of the abridged editions, the dialogue goes like this:

> *"Die!" exclaimed Marius.*
> *"Yes, but that is nothing," said Jean Valjean.*
> *Cosette uttered a piercing cry: "Father! Father!*
> *You shall live. You are going to live. I will have you*
> *live, do you hear!"*
> *Jean Valjean raised his head towards her with*
> *adoration. "Oh, yes, forbid me to die. Who knows? I*
> *shall obey perhaps. I was just dying when you came.*
> *That stopped me, it seemed to me that I was born*
> *again!"*

But Jean Valjean dies a few minutes later.

When I first heard the lyrics sung in this scene during the musical at the Auditorium Theater in Chicago, the strikingly similar words of Scott and Valerie instantly came to mind. As Cosette was guileless toward her father, so Scott and Val were guileless in their vehement assertions that their father must not die. They loved me unconditionally; they wanted me to stay around forever; reason was totally obscured by a love I didn't understand.

The touching words in the emotionally-charged last scene of *Les Miz* have continued to bring tears to the eyes of theater-goers everywhere. And I am no exception. For me, the final scene always triggers tears and stifled sobs right through the curtain call. Over the years, every time I played the audio cassette of the musical, read the book, or watched one of the film versions of *Les Miserables*, that final scene has never failed to produce tears—and, I am convinced, inner healing. Through the daily faith practice of contemplative prayer, I am learning to accept God's unconditional love for me. The more I accept His love, the more aware I am that God is doing a deep, healing work.

That is why the Bishop and Jean Valjean continue to be my heroes. Both of them were unconditional lovers; both had a good measure of that all-important gift—the first fruit of the Spirit—love. Their stories in *Les Miz* had a big part in prompting me to faithfully continue contemplative prayer, to allow God to dazzle me with His presence, and to accept His total acceptance of me.

The inner healing that has occurred through these experiences has been accompanied by a generous portion of the gift of love. How wonderful it is to begin to see everyone as precious. How wonderful it is that I am now able to look people in the eye and say, "I love you." How wonderful it is to close a phone call to a family member or friend with an "I love you," without gagging and feeling like a phony!

How wonderful it is to know that there are some people in my life whom I don't want to see die. How wonderful it is to experience an incredible "lightness of being"—to not take myself so seriously. How wonderful it is to know I am accepted, and because I know, I can spontaneously smile even when there is no special reason to do so.

In the next chapter, I share a couple of additional experiences I had with family members which God used to teach me the wonder of unconditional love.

8

ANOTHER LIFE-CHANGING ENCOUNTER

There is nothing you and I can do for the Lord that He could not get someone else to do. He could raise up sons and daughters to Abraham out of the field stones and give them the talent, the inspiration, and the grace to carry out all our tasks.

There is only one thing that you and I can give to the Lord that absolutely no one else can ever give Him. He dreamed about it, as it were, from all eternity, when He thought of creating us. If we do not give it to Him, He will never get it. In this He has made Himself a beggar. For He truly wants what we have to give, yet He can get it only if we decide freely to give it to Him.

What is this one thing—the one thing necessary? It is our personal love. This is what God made us for: to lavish the joy of His love upon us, which can be received only with love, the love that returns to Him our personal love. No one else can ever give Him our personal love. If we do not give it to Him, He will never receive this particular love—which He wants!

As one of the great mystics of the sixteenth century put it, "When the evening of life comes, we will be judged on love." How else can a God who is love judge? Therefore, even for those of us who are called to an active ministry, it is essential that we spend enough time at the feet of the Master.

—*M. Basil Pennington*

8

ANOTHER
LIFE-CHANGING
ENCOUNTER

Over ten years ago, in 1985, I received an ominous phone call from my oldest daughter, Vicki, that went something like this: "Dad, I want to come over to talk to you—alone."

The confidential tone to her voice made it clear to me that no questions were to be asked. So I only said, "Mom isn't here—come on over right now."

Vicki and her husband, Greg, lived in Glen Ellyn, the same suburb of Chicago where both had grown up and where both sets of parents and most of their extended family and friends still live. Greg's apartment-rental business was located in an adjoining town. They were a typical suburban family with two children—Valerie and Shawn—and the traditional cat and dog. Their special claim to uniqueness was their all-consuming interest in sailing. They owned a small sailboat, which they docked in Lake Geneva, about 60 miles northwest of Chicago.

While I waited for Vicki to arrive, I speculated on what the big secret might be. I didn't have a clue—but like most parents in such circumstances, I anticipated "bad" news rather than "good" news.

Vicki was the first of the four children that Marge and I adopted over a period of six years. (Our fifth child was born to us after we had been married for 19 years.) We adopted Vicki when she was six weeks old. When we saw her for the first time at the adoption agency, we didn't have any trouble making up our minds. She was beautiful! Our only question was, "What's her name?"

The agency worker responded, "She has no name—but we call her Candy, because she's so sweet."

We officially named her Victoria Susan and called her Vicki, but we have never stopped seeing her as Candy, because she's always been a real sweetheart. None of our children was easier to raise. She didn't even go through the terrible two's or terrible teens!

When Vicki arrived at our apartment that day, she and I sat down in the family room. Knowing that I'm a no-nonsense-just-give-me-the-facts kind of dad, Vicki immediately blurted out the whole story in a few sentences, without any interruption from me.

"Dad, we've decided to take the big plunge, and I wanted you to be the first to know. We've decided to sell our house and leave Glen Ellyn. We've already ordered a 41' Lord Nelson sailboat, and we intend to make the boat our home. Who knows, maybe we'll sail around the world. In any event, our only definite plans are to go to the Caribbean, then to South America, and then on to Europe. We expect to home-school the children and be away for quite a few years."

My immediate response was short and direct: "Honey, go for it. It sounds great to me. You're young, and since that's your dream, now's the time to do it." Though I hadn't anticipated anything quite so abrupt and radical, I wasn't too surprised either. They had rented a large sailboat in the Bahamas for six weeks the previous Fall, though nothing had been said at the time about any long-range plans.

I don't remember much about the rest of our discussion, but since I was genuinely happy for them, I presume I was reasonably positive in my response.

However, I do remember how the end of our conversation went. At one point I asked, "Isn't it kind of dangerous to try to cross the Atlantic in a little sailboat? I'm afraid that Mom and I will probably spend a lot of time worrying about you. What would we do if something happened to you?"

After attempting to allay my concern, Vicki looked me square in the eye and said, "Would you cry if something happened to me?"

What a question to ask—and to answer! I was at a loss to know how to reply, but finally said something innocuous like, "I'm not sure I would cry, but it sure would be awful."

After a long pause, Vicki finally spoke. "You mean you wouldn't cry?" she asked with an incredulous look. When a clear-cut answer was not forthcoming from me, huge tears slowly gathered in the corner of her eyes and began to roll down her beautiful face.

I froze. I didn't say or do anything. I wish I could say that I gathered her in my arms, hugged her, kissed her and reassured her. But I did nothing and said nothing. I guess my stoic, unemotional, untouching German background left me little room to even consider future tears over such an unlikely possibility. All I could do was make a couple of lame comments about how awful it would be.

I was so numb from that encounter that to this day I can't remember what else happened or what else was said as Vicki left our apartment. But I realized there was something radically wrong with me. I knew I had wounded my daughter deeply by not reassuring her with the words she needed to hear. Her question had taken me completely by surprise, and I'd been helpless to respond appropriately.

It wasn't until three years later, when I heard the John Bradshaw TV lectures on dysfunctionality, that I faced squarely into the truth: Bill Volkman knew little about love—unconditional love—and practically nothing about how to express it to his world. He was a classic case of dysfunctionality; no one can even begin to function as a reasonably whole person if he does not know how to receive and give love.

Yes, I had plenty of plaques, citations and letters of commendation in my closet attesting to my forty years of dedicated "Martha" service to dozens of Christian organizations. And no wonder. Because of their pressing "needs," most churches and not-for-profit organizations are all too ready to enlist well-intentioned, well-heeled, do-gooder professionals like me.

The first words on a citation I received from a Christian college that named a building after me pretty much tells my "do-gooder" story: "Outstanding gentleman and college professor, respected attorney and successful businessman, energetic builder and strategic planner for our College, active participant in many Christian organizations and Christian youth movements, builder of our College's multipurpose unit, gifted planner of our beautiful campus, man whose vision, concern, and drive made possible the new campus building," etc., etc.

Sounds impressive, doesn't it? But Paul gives us these sobering words in I Corinthians 13: "If I speak with the tongues of angels...and know all mysteries...and if I have all faith...but do not have *love*, I am nothing. And if I give all my possessions...and if I deliver my body to be burned...but do not have *love*, it profits me nothing."

The preceding verses have indicted me throughout the years. And I have also struggled with the following two verses. First, the words of Solomon: "Unless the Lord builds the house, they labor in vain who build it." The other verse was Jesus' own words: "By this all will know you are My disciples, if you have love for one another."

Throughout all my years of dedicated Christian service,

there had always been one major ingredient in short supply in my life: unconditional love. Deep down I knew that I couldn't look at anyone without judging them. I couldn't see anyone as perfect in Christ. I was more interested in seeing their performance improve than in accepting or loving them as they are.

As I mentioned in an earlier chapter, the turning point in my life came at age 65, when I added silent, contemplative prayer to my regular prayer routine. During the first couple of years of practicing centering prayer God began a healing from within, filling me with a love for all people and all things that is much deeper and more far-reaching than I could ever have imagined. I found that God's promise is true: those who wait on the Lord will not be disappointed. God cannot lie. Healing and transformation come as we faithfully practice His presence.

But as so often happens, we don't really "get" what God is saying to us until He sends one or more messengers to help clarify the message. My precious daughter, Vicki, had been one of my first messengers. My encounter with her had made me face into my total inability to express my love to her and to others.

Another such messenger was Vicki's son, Shawn. In 1991, Vicki and Greg's sailboat, the *Shaval*, was docked in Puerta La Cruz, Venezuela. Marge and I had flown down to visit with them for two weeks. Vicki had rented a dockside condo for us, because the boat was a bit crowded and she knew I get queasy on boats, especially when they're still tied up.

My grandson Shawn was twelve years old at the time. Since he and I hadn't seen each other for almost a year, we spent almost every waking hour of my vacation together.

One day Shawn asked me to go with him to his room on the boat so he could show me some "treasures" he had collected. Passing first by his sister's room, Shawn pointed to a picture on the wall and said, "That's my favorite picture of you, Papa." I was surprised to see it was our wedding picture taken during World War II when I was only 20 years old. Marge was in her floral wedding dress, and I was in my Navy "whites." I remember thinking to myself: *How strange. Why would Shawn's favorite picture of me be one that was taken over 30 years before he was even born?*

When we came to his room, Shawn shuffled through various items in his dresser drawer, but finally showed me just one thing. With a sheepish grin, he held up a large metal button. It read, "I love my Grampa." I gulped, hugged him and, without a word, we walked out of the room hand in hand. *Why would Shawn ask to show me his important collectibles and then show me just one metal button?*

Later that day, we all crowded into a dilapidated taxi to go to town. As Shawn got into the back seat he said, "Here, sit next to me, Papa." He immediately held my hand.

Marge squeezed in the back seat beside me. Feeling a bit cramped, I remarked, "I sure would like to lose a few pounds."

My grandson immediately reacted: "No, Papa, I don't want you to lose any weight! Please don't lose any weight! You're just right the way you are!"

"But," I protested, "I don't want to lose a lot, Shawn—just a little. I just know that I'd feel better if I were ten pounds lighter."

"I don't know about that," Shawn responded, "all I know is that I'll always love you just the way you are!"

Just the way you are! He loves me just the way I am! As he squeezed my hand, I gulped again.

Early the next morning, as I sat alone on the balcony of our condo for my "centering" time, I reflected in detail on Shawn's comments and actions of the previous day.

Suddenly, tears started to flow and love seemed to envelop me. It all became very clear. Shawn loved me unconditionally! God truly loved me unconditionally. God had used Shawn's love as another object lesson for me. Finally, I could accept that God loved me unconditionally—making it possible for me to love Him and others as never before.

A couple of years later Vicki returned home for a visit. This time I called her, and without explanation I said, "Vicki, I'd like to talk to you—alone! Could you come over?"

A few minutes later we were sitting in the same chairs in the same family room as we had some years earlier. After refreshing her recollection of our discussion of about seven years before, I brought her up to date on God's inner healing in my life as a result of my deepening intimate relationship with the Lord through centering prayer.

Then I knelt down in front of Vicki, gently cupped her tanned cheeks in my hands, looked directly into her eyes, and said, "I want you to know, Vicki, that I love you very much. I've always loved you. Unfortunately, for many years I couldn't tell you or show you adequately. But now I want you to make me a promise. I want you to promise me to live very carefully—on the high seas and everywhere else—because if something happens to you I *would* cry, and I don't know if I would ever stop crying!"

As I spoke, large tears gathered in her eyes. For just a moment I had the horrible thought that I had blundered and that once again I was hurting her. The tears began to flow down her cheeks and over my index fingers. But as I watched them fall, I relaxed, as I realized that this time she was smiling! She was crying for joy. Now she knew for certain that her dad loved her.

Because I had begun to experience God's unconditional love for me through some of God's special messengers and through my centering prayer times, I had finally been healed enough to be able to express my love to my precious daughter.

9

LOOKING AT
THE HEART

When the time to be before the Lord has come, know that your friend "faith," and your friend "intention," will guide and conduct you to God. You arrive there by means of an act of faith and by perfect resignation on your part as you wait in His presence.

If you do not retract your faith and your intention, then you walk in faith and resignation, and therefore you walk in prayer.

A mountain does not say, "I am a mountain." Nor does a woman walk around saying, "I am married, I am a wife, I am a wife." Do you walk around saying, "I am a Christian, I am a Christian"? If you never think about it, still you are a Christian. The woman is a wife and the mountain is a mountain.

The Christian is obligated to do no more than this: to believe more with his heart than he does with his mouth. The wife gives a demonstration of her fidelity to her husband by the very life she lives. Once the Christian has resolved to believe that the Lord dwells within him, and that he will henceforth seek the Lord, and do nothing but what he does through God ... once that has been done, the Christian should rest ... satisfied in the faith that is in his spirit.

—*Michael Molinos*

9

LOOKING AT
THE HEART

There are many liberating secrets that God has graciously revealed to me during my lifelong spiritual journey. And this has been especially true over the past few years since waiting on God in silence has become such a vital part of my devotional time. The secret of "the pure intent of the heart" is a very recent revelation for me. The realization that God judges us (or should I say, accepts us) on the basis of our core commitment rather than on the basis of performance is a liberating secret indeed.

I know now, beyond any doubt, that God at all times sees my heart's intention to love Him and His world, without keeping score of my performance. But it has been easier to accept this for myself than to stop being a scorekeeper on everybody around me. The truth is that at times I rather enjoy being critical—and with all my practice, I'm pretty good at it!

Hebrews 4:12 has long been a favorite verse of mine. In the past I have focused primarily on the first part of the verse: "For the word of God is living and active and sharper than any two-edged sword, and piercing as far as the division of soul and spirit...." To me that meant that if I knew enough Scripture, I would be able to distinguish between soul and spirit in everyday life.

We all have asked ourselves questions like, "What is the will of God for me in this situation?" Or after a handling a difficult situation: "Was I right or wrong? Was I walking in the Spirit, or being manipulated by the flesh?"

For years I thought that the answer to such questions could only be found in Scriptural imperatives. The phrase, "the word of God," meant only one thing to me: the Bible. I wanted to have a proof-text for every conceivable situation. I thought that I could be like the "adequate, equipped" person in II Timothy 3—if I knew the Scriptures well enough, then I would know the will of God. I could go around wielding my "two-edged sword" like a scalpel that properly divides the bone from the marrow—instead of a meat cleaver which indiscriminately chops up everything in its path.

Needless to say, my attempts to discern the will of God by the use of Scripture alone failed. With the best of intentions, my use of the scalpel had the same effect as if I was wielding that meat cleaver. Trying to use it as a scalpel on myself and my world left me confused and hurting, and I left a lot of wounded family members and friends in my wake. I learned that bashing myself or others with Scripture does nothing to reveal the love of God to me or to them.

The Law is a good schoolmaster, but it was designed only to point the way to Christ—to be a stepping-stone to a higher, simpler, better law: the Royal Law of Love. We must turn from the law of sin and death to the Law of Life; from codified right and wrong to the One who embodies righteousness; from the letter of the law to the Spirit of the Law; from the tree of the knowledge of good and evil to the Tree of Life; from the outer, written word to the indwelling Word.

On a recent trip to London, one of our grandchildren on the trip with us asked me whether he should give money to the many people begging at the "tube" stations and on the busy streets. He didn't know how to express his dilemma, but what he was really wondering was, "How do we know when sharing with the needy is the right thing to do, and when it is just a sentimental gesture that might do more harm than good?" Before attempting to answer his question I shared a true story with him.

A friend of mine struggled for many years over when and how much he should give to beggars and street-people. One day he saw something which he said irrevocably changed his thinking about sharing with every needy person he met. From a distance he observed a beggar pull a compact cellular phone from inside his coat and dial a call. It crossed his mind that the man might be calling his broker! My friend told me that since that time he has refused to allow himself to share with the poor, because he is afraid that he might give to someone who is not really needy.

"But God isn't a scorekeeper," I explained to my grandchildren. "He doesn't keep a list of the things we do or don't do—He only looks at our hearts. Whenever we share out of real compassion with one of God's children, we are giving to Christ. What that person does with our gift is not our responsibility. If we harden our hearts to every poor person we see, we may be hardening our hearts to God."

I want my grandchildren to know something I didn't know at their age: that God sees our hearts, and that He knows our intentions; and that even though we don't always live up to them, He is not mad at us. He looks on us with loving compassion and sees only our deepest, inner motives.

Many of us were raised in a cold, critical, religious atmosphere in which God is seen as a scorekeeper and a judge, dispensing rewards and punishment in direct proportion to our performance—"whatsoever a person sows, that also shall he reap." Everything is cause and effect, tit for tat.

Certainly, Scripture has this side to it. But, what about grace? Isn't the overriding *good news* of the Scriptures that we have a God who does not judge us based on performance? We are His precious children, His beloved Spouse—created for love and intimacy with Him for all eternity, starting now—and we are on a long spiritual journey. During that journey, from beginning to end, He totally accepts us, loves us and urges us on, just like a parent with a toddler. How liberating such unconditional love is. What a relief it is to learn that we have always been objectively judged by the intent of our heart rather than being judged subjectively based on our performance.

I am just beginning to understand why Jesus advised, "Do not judge according to appearance, but judge with righteous judgment" (John 7:24); and why Paul said, "...from now on we recognize no one according to the flesh" (II Cor. 5:16). We are to see all Christians as new creations in Christ, and to see all others in terms of their full potential in Christ. As one who has spent the better part of a lifetime trying to straighten out his wife, his family, and his local world, I can say from experience that such a seeing comes only as a special gift from God!

We are meant to be affirmers, not evaluators. Affirmers, relying on gentleness and understanding, are able to bring out the best in everyone. Evaluators, on the other hand, resort to judgment and criticism, which inevitably degenerates into condemnation, then rejection, and finally hatred. By hindsight, it's now clear to me that I have spent altogether too much of my life being an evaluator, a prosecutor, a judge, jury and warden for my immediate family and for many others I felt I had to control or "fix."

But by God's grace, just as I have come to realize that He has always seen beyond my erratic performance to my core intention, so, in turn, I have learned a little about seeing the heart intentions of my family, my friends and my world.

As my precious grandchildren reach their teen years, sooner or later they all find it necessary to learn by the negative—they all experiment with habits and lifestyles that I would not choose for them. Though I know it is necessary for them to cut the umbilical cord to their families and learn to make choices on their own, I still wince and worry about some of those choices. Over and over again, I lapse back into judging by appearances.

A recent episode involving my oldest grandson taught me a lot about the importance of seeing through to the intentions of the heart.

Questionable results in two routine medical tests during my latest annual physical suddenly had my doctor talking about the strong possibility of prostate cancer. We all concluded that a biopsy of the prostate was the next necessary procedure.

Though Marge and I shared our concern at that point with our five children—because they love us, and for prayer and moral support—we asked them to say nothing about it to any of the grandchildren, lest we upset them needlessly. Later, when the biopsy gave me a clean bill of health, we immediately shared the good news.

That afternoon our son, Scott, told his son, Brian, the details about my prostate cancer scare. Brian's reaction went something like this: "Dad, why didn't you tell me about Papa sooner? If I had known, I would have skipped school and driven down to Glen Ellyn to be with him. Papa shouldn't have had to go through this all alone!"

Scott was incredulous. "You mean you would have taken off from school and driven 300 miles just to be there? What would you do?"

"I'd just be there with Papa. He shouldn't have been alone! Now I wish I had spent more time with him when I worked for him last summer!"

"But, Brian, there's nothing you could have done. What would you have done if you had gone down there?"

"I'd have ... just hung out with him," he replied lamely.

After Scott told me of his conversation with Brian, I tried to share the details with Marge. It took me a long time to recount the dialogue to her, as I would choke up and could not continue. I was greatly touched by what Brian had said. *If I'd known, I would have driven to Glen Ellyn ... Papa shouldn't have been alone ... I would just be with him ... I'd have just hung out with him.*

During the past four years, Brian had changed considerably. He'd grown from 5'2" to 5'10." He had also been going through his share of typical teenage rebellion. The wonderful, affectionate boy I'd seen so much of had become a reserved young man whom I seldom saw. I had wondered what was happening to my caring, sensitive grandson!

I suddenly saw that the problem had been more mine than his. I was judging Brian by how he *appeared* to me, rather than by his inner intentions. His heart hadn't changed; he was just growing up and trying out his wings. In his heart he still responded with love. In a crucial moment, nothing was more important to Brian than to "hang out" with someone he loves. Despite all my talk about "seeing through," I had found it difficult when my precious teenage grandson didn't meet all my expectations.

This experience shattered my confidence in my ability to judge people by appearances. It reinforced my desire and my resolve to stop keeping score—and to start seeing my world from the inside out. I was fed up with my old ways; I wanted to see things as God does. I wanted to look at each person in my world not by what they do, but by who they are—by their deepest inner motives, by their core commitment, by the *intent* of their hearts.

10

INTENTION
AND ATTENTION

I know a person who for forty years has practiced the presence of God, to which he gives several other names. Sometimes he calls it a simple act—a clear and distinct knowledge of God; and sometimes he calls it a vague view or a general and loving look at God—a remembrance of Him. He also refers to it as attention to God, silent communion with God, confidence in God, or the life and the peace of the soul.

To sum it up, this person has told me that all these manners of the presence of God are synonyms which signify the same thing, which have all become natural to him. The presence of God is the concentration of the soul's attention on God, remembering that He is always present.

My friend says that by dwelling in the presence of God he has established such a sweet communion with the Lord that His spirit abides, without much effort, in the restful peace of God. In this rest, he is filled with faith that equips him to handle anything that comes to him.

This is what he calls the "actual presence" of God, which includes any and all kinds of communion a person who still dwells on the earth can possibly have with God in heaven. At times, he can live as if no one else existed on earth but himself and God. He lovingly speaks with God wherever he goes, asking Him for all he needs and rejoicing with Him in a thousand ways.

—*Brother Lawrence*

10

INTENTION
AND ATTENTION

When I was first confronted with the concept of silent, contemplative prayer, three major objections to it immediately leapt to mind. Firstly, "Isn't this silence a waste of time?"; secondly, "I just can't keep my mind from racing"; and thirdly, "Isn't it dangerous to just sit there and think about nothing?"

As a lawyer and businessman, I was especially sensitive to the first objection: that wordless prayer is so much wasted time. My training taught me that time is money, so there wasn't any room for waste. I evaluated everything on the basis of whether or not it was useful, with practical consequences and measurable results.

In the past, the story of Mary of Bethany *wasting* a bottle of expensive ointment on Jesus had always been a challenge to me. Jesus explained what was going on, and I accepted it—but it wasn't something that I could easily translate into my own life. Remember the way Judas reacted? He was indignant. He didn't understand that Mary was recklessly in love with the Master—and that lovers don't count the cost. The object of their love is all that matters to them.

It was the same Mary—the sister of Martha and Lazarus—who didn't think it was a waste of time to sit in awe at the feet of Jesus, while Martha was doing all the work in the kitchen. Jesus settled the issue of the relative importance of "doing" and "being" once and for all when He told Martha that she "fretted" and "fussed" instead of choosing the "one necessary thing," which was to be with Him.

When we practice God's presence in centering prayer, our intention is precisely this: to *do* nothing. Our only desire is to *be* with our Lover, to "hang out" with Him. We are responding to Christ's gentle plea: "Behold, I stand at the door and knock; if anyone hears My voice and opens the door, I will come in to him, and will dine with him, and he with Me." And a long, leisurely dining experience with our Lover is never a waste of time.

My second major objection to contemplative prayer was that I couldn't keep my mind from racing. I concluded that I just wasn't any good at wordless prayer. My mind seemed to go off in a dozen different directions. In spite of all my good intentions to be "attentive to Christ's presence," 14 minutes out of a 15-minute centering time seemed to be spent either on a problem at my motel, on an idea about one of my investments in the stock market, on a thought about a later appointment, or even on a tantalizing spiritual insight (which I was afraid I would forget if I didn't get up and write it down immediately).

I had to realize that all this is perfectly normal—the mind was made to think, just as the body was made to breathe. The secret is to let the thoughts go and not worry about them. Centering is not a technique to quiet the mind; it's a way of entering into the quiet that is already there, buried under the fifty thousand thoughts which an average person thinks each day. Our union and communion take place at a level far deeper than our mind.

I had to learn experientially the important truth that God is not a scorekeeper. If my intention is to be attentive to His presence, He is more than delighted. He does not analyze or judge our performance! We may; He does not. Our heartfelt attempt to come to Him and to be with Him in response to His inner initiative in us is all that He asks of anyone. The story of the prodigal son gives us a picture of a loving father who daily searches the horizon for a sign of the return of his beloved son. That father's heart is like God's— He is totally thrilled with us, especially when we turn towards Him.

My third objection, when I first attempted centering prayer, was that "it might be dangerous to just sit there thinking about nothing." In my Charismatic days, I had heard many dire warnings about the countless demons who were ever ready to take over the mind of anyone whose thoughts were not sufficiently focused on Christ and His written Word.

But I soon learned that the practice of contemplative prayer was not meant to be a time of "thinking about nothing" or an "emptying of the mind," as critics suggest. Rather, we come to God in love, to be fully attentive to His presence within. We can't "empty the mind" of thoughts—that's impossible. But we can choose to pay attention to the God who dwells within us and not pay attention to the endless thoughts that crowd our minds. We don't come to cram more concepts about Him into our minds; our sole purpose is to allow our minds and hearts to be filled to the full with an awareness of the great mystery of God: Christ in us, our hope of glory.

In *The Wink of Faith*, I emphasized the importance of A and A—acknowledgment and affirmation: keep *acknowledging* to yourself with words and concepts who you are in Christ, and keep *affirming* others as to who lives in them. I still think that this is good advice.

But I want to repeat again that devotional activities

and sharing with others—all our talking, prayer, study, reading, acknowledging, affirming and the rest—should be complemented by a little time each day to engage in silent contemplation, in wordless prayer, in basking in His presence. For this, I emphasize I and A—intention and attention. Our *intention* is to take some time each day to give full *attention* to the presence of our indwelling Lover, the One who is our Husband at the deepest ground of our being—the One to whom we are Bride.

Because of my short memory and my endless preoccupations with the minutiae of life, God had to use a special object lesson on me to make me more consistently aware of who I am as the spouse of Christ.

I have never audibly heard God speak to me about anything, but He has, on rare occasions, clearly revealed His will to me in an irrefutable way. It comes as an instantaneous clear impression in my mind.

About three years ago, this is what came: "Because you have such a short memory of My indwelling presence, go out and buy a second wedding ring. You have one on your left hand as a symbol of your marriage to Marge; now buy one for your right hand as a symbol and reminder of your spiritual marriage to Me."

Needless to say, when I "heard" that communication, I was dumbfounded. What a strange, "ridiculous" request!

I had read somewhere that most nuns wear a wedding band on their right hand as a symbol of their marriage to Christ, but *Why me, Lord*? It seemed so goofy (and potentially embarrassing) that for six months I procrastinated about buying the ring, though I periodically checked with the Lord to see if I had heard Him right. His answer was always the same, "Yes, you heard Me right!"

But a bit of background is necessary to understand why God's simple request was so hard for me.

My son, Scott, and I had operated a coin shop for ten years, buying and selling gold and silver bullion, as well as coins. We started the business late in 1979 when the price of both silver and gold were skyrocketing. The price of silver jumped from $5 to $54 an ounce; gold moved from $400 to $850 an ounce. People waited in line to sell scrap silver and gold of every kind, including old wedding bands left over from broken marriages.

Every few weeks, I drove sixty miles to sell scrap gold and silver to a big dealer in Indiana who dealt in turn with a refinery. One day this dealer said to me, "Come into my back room, Bill. I want to show you something." The room was loaded with boxes, bags, and piles of coins, scrap gold and silver. Pointing to a coin bag on the floor, he said, "Check out that bag."

I reached into the bag and scooped out a handful of gold wedding bands. He commented casually, "That's some of the wedding rings I've collected over the past couple of months. That represents a lot of divorces and heartaches!" My guess is that the bag contained at least two thousand 14-karat gold bands.

Having seen so many used wedding bands while engaged in the coin and precious metals business, the idea of going to a retail store and paying full price bothered me. I was also loath to buy a used band from any of my former competitors, as I was afraid that they might ask me, "What's it for?" Somehow I felt they might not understand my explanation!

But after six long months of vacillation, without receiving even a bit of sympathy from the Lord about my dilemma, I did go to one of my former competitors. To make a long story short, he sold me a new ring wholesale for $60, no questions asked.

So now I wear two wedding bands: one as a reminder of my human marriage, and the other one as an ever-present reminder of my eternal marriage to Christ. It reminds me of His ever-abiding, indwelling presence, and is a symbol of my intention to give my Spouse the attention He desires and deserves.

Now, if anyone asks me why I wear two wedding bands, I am more than willing to provide a detailed explanation!

11

THE TREE OF
UNKNOWING

The great Thomas Aquinas, toward the end of his life, wouldn't write and wouldn't talk; he had seen the glory of God. I had thought he kept that famous silence of his for only a couple of months, but it went on for years. He realized he had made a fool of himself, and he said so explicitly.

The highest form of talking about the Trinity is to know that one does not know—to know God as unknown. St. Thomas even says, as unknowable.

Reality, God, divinity, truth, and love are all unknowable; that means they cannot be comprehended by the thinking mind. That would set at rest so many questions people have, because we're always living under the illusion that we know. We don't. We cannot know.

The fact is that you're surrounded by God and yet you don't see God, because you "know" about Him. The final barrier to the vision of God is our God concept. You miss God because you think you know. That's the terrible thing about religion. That's what the Gospels were saying—that religious people "knew," so they got rid of Jesus. The highest knowledge of God is to know God as unknowable.

—*Anthony de Mello*

11

THE TREE OF UNKNOWING

Part of the legal defense used by a recently convicted murderer of an abortion doctor was justifiable homicide—his killing was justified because "God told me to do it." It seems that the person convicted was 100% convinced that all abortions are murder and that, therefore, all doctors performing abortions are murderers who deserve to die.

The rationale of believing that the same God who says, "Thou shalt not kill," would desire the murder of any doctor who performs abortions eludes me, as it probably does most of us. In any event, thinking about the extreme position taken by this particular "born-again" Christian, as well as about comments made by various observers on both sides of the abortion issue, has caused me to consider again how one determines the will of God in any given situation. It has also forced me to re-evaluate my personal understanding of Christian liberty and responsibility.

Is there a specific Scriptural answer for every theological, cultural and ethical question that confronts us—capital punishment, eternal security, homosexuality, pacifism, women priests and pastors, the proper day for Sabbath observance, etc.? Can anyone *objectively* and categorically know the will of God concerning the various decisions we must make every day, some of which involve hotly debated areas of theology and personal conduct? Will we ever be delivered from the questioning, the doubts, the conflicts and the anguish which is a part of all those questions and their answers?

The Apostle Paul gives us his answer to these questions: "Let each one be fully convinced in his own mind" (Rom. 14:5). Granted, the Apostle was primarily talking about whether a particular day of the week should be revered more than any other, but based on the general tenor of this chapter on Christian liberty, I would assume that Paul believed that personal conviction is the only proper basis for all such decisions.

This conclusion of Paul's may not be dogmatic enough for many of us. He puts the responsibility right back in our own hands, clearly stating that the decision is ours, based on our faith in God and our personal relationship with Him. Even with regard to questions that many would consider "not debatable," the same principle still applies—grace demands that we allow others to live according to their conscience, within the limits of the law of the land.

We were not meant to live only by objective standards, by the letter of the Law; as mature Christians, we live by the Spirit—the heart—of the Law. Our Trinity is not Father, Son and Holy *Scripture*, but Father, Son and Holy *Spirit*. We are to live by the promptings of faith, not by rigid formulas.

So my specific answers to the three earlier questions are simple and consistent: No, No and No. Scripture is not a specific "how-to" manual, though it contains extremely helpful principles to aid us in reaching personal decisions. No one can objectively know the will of God for everyone else. And none of us will ever be free from the anguish of "not knowing."

In this life we are not meant to be free from questions, doubts and conflicts—the anguish of "not knowing." "Not knowing" is a part of the human condition. I continue to be amazed at how many U.S. Supreme Court decisions are made on a 5 to 4 vote. Time and time again, one swing vote determines the outcome of monumental decisions which affect the lives of millions.

It's not just the tenuousness of these decisions that amazes me, but the fact that some of the best-informed, best-trained and most experienced jurists in the world cannot agree. Change one vote, and the law of the land goes in a different direction. How can anyone dogmatically say, "I know," and then make it even worse by adding, "And if you conclude differently, you are wrong"?

A few years ago, author and Roman Catholic priest Andrew Greeley wrote a position paper (published in *The Critic* magazine) entitled "How Just A War?" on the morality of the Gulf War. He wrote:

> *In terms of the just-war tradition, I deem the war to be immoral not because the cause was unjust but because all peaceful means had not been exhausted, because the force was disproportionate, and because more harm was done than good accomplished.*

He goes on to say:

> *I am convinced that history will judge Bush and Cheney and their advisers as war criminals and the American people, with all their flags and yellow ribbons, as guilty of complicity in war crimes.*

Though the vast majority of Americans probably disagree with his conclusion, that does not prove that they are right and Greeley is wrong. For me, the brilliance of his paper is found in his concluding statement—

> *In a complex world and in a civil and pluralistic society, there does not seem to be a reasonable alternative to moral humility.*

And I believe Greeley is right. The key is "moral humility." We can passionately disagree with each other in our "application of principles to gray, complex and problematic reality," but we must always be prepared to admit that we might be wrong.

In psychiatrist M. Scott Peck's recent book, *Further Along the Road Less Traveled*, he makes this blunt admission: "I don't know anything." He adds, "But the real truth of the matter is that you don't know anything either. None of us does. We dwell in a profoundly mysterious universe." Having been converted to Christianity a couple of years after completing *The Road Less Traveled*, Peck has obviously been led to a most important conclusion: we are meant to live by faith, not just by rational knowledge and our intellect.

How often have you heard (and said) the words: "I *know* I'm right!" Not only are we convinced that we are right, but often we are also convinced that anyone who takes a different position must be wrong. Few of us are prepared to say with M. Scott Peck: "I don't know!"

So, where does all this leave us? It leaves us confused, frustrated and discouraged—we are at our wit's end. Good! Finally God has us exactly where He wants us— hopeless, helpless and poor in spirit. We are stuck with only one answer: living by faith. It seems that most of us will not turn to God until we first come to the end of ourselves. Experiencing the kingdom of heaven does not become our portion until we learn to turn within and live by faith.

Jesus challenged the knowers of all ages with these words: "You search the Scriptures, because you think that in them you have eternal life...[but] you are unwilling to come to Me, that you may have life" (John 5:39-40). There are many Christians today who continue to look to the letter of Scripture for their answers and their spiritual life, instead of coming to the Spirit of Christ that dwells within them and trusting by faith that He will lead them into all truth.

The only alternative to a life of rules, objective truth and formulas based on reason and "knowing" is a life of "not knowing"—a life of faith, a life of waiting on God in silence and listening, a life of walking in the Spirit. It's when we finally choose the faith walk, admitting that we do not know, that we can rely on the prophecy of Isaiah when he says that our "ears will hear a word...turn to the right or to the left" (30:21).

My own experience confirms this. The longer I walk in faith and consistently acknowledge my beloved Spouse by waiting on Him in silence, the more I "hear" Him and sense His leading in the details of everyday life. Now, instead of agonizing over every situation, I rest in Him, aware of His involvement in the myriad of daily decisions, and excited beyond imagination about each new day as it unfolds.

Like Adam and Eve, we all have been given the same basic commandment: "From any tree of the garden you may eat freely; but from the tree of the knowledge of good and evil you shall not eat." But, like Adam and Eve, most of us continue to make the mistake of choosing to eat of the fruit of the tree of knowledge, or tree of *knowing*, instead of in faith taking from the Tree of Life, the Tree of *Unknowing*.

God had told Adam and Eve that eating of the tree of knowledge would result in death. Living by the Law brings death, because we become proud ("I know I'm right!) and judgmental ("If you disagree with me, you must be wrong"). When our source of faith is the tree of knowing, we miss the Tree of Life. Knowing, without humility, means we don't know that we don't know. We think we have all the answers, so there is no room for paradoxes, no room for either/or, no room for mystery, and no room for an ineffable God.

Understandably, most of us find that embracing an unknowable (beyond human understanding), ineffable (incapable of being described in words), inscrutable (mysterious, incapable of being understood), incomprehensible, unfathomable, unutterable, indescribable and unintelligible God is a bit scary. Knowing an ineffable God is an oxymoron to the rational mind, but when seen through the eye of faith it can be embraced along with all the other paradoxes and mysteries of life.

Seeking to "know God" is not the same as taking from the tree of knowledge of good and evil—it is, instead, taking from the Tree of Life. Paul's longing to know Christ is clear in the familiar Philippians text: "That I might know Him and the power of His resurrection...." But it is clear that he was speaking of a subjective heart knowing, not an objective head knowing.

James Finley, in his book, *Merton's Palace of Nowhere*, reminds us that, like God, we are to a certain extent, beyond time, space and matter, because He (the Unknowable) is our life. God is beyond precise description—He cannot be contained in a word, or in a group of words—He is nothing (no "thing"), nowhere (no "where") and nobody (no "body"). Hid in Christ, alive in the heavenly kingdom, the same is true of us. Finley writes, "And so no matter what we have it is always enough, for nothing is enough. No matter where we are, we are nowhere. No matter who we become we are nobody."

Humans have never liked the idea of "not knowing."

When a blind man was brought to Jesus for healing, the disciples immediately asked the question: "Who sinned, this man or his parents?" The disciples still assumed that life was always the rational product of cause and effect. But Jesus' startling answer must have jarred them to reconsider, when He said, "No one sinned," going on to explain that the man was born blind "that God might be glorified." God glorified by this poor man's blindness? What kind of a God is that? But Paul vetoes such presumptuous questioning when he bluntly retorts: "Shall the thing formed say to Him that formed it, 'Why did you make me like this?'" (See Romans 9:20.)

In light of Romans 8:26-27, we should welcome "not knowing," especially when it comes to praying for ourselves and others. "For we do not know how to pray as we should, but the Spirit Himself intercedes for us...according to the will of God."

Imagine, whenever we perceive a special need and are led to pray for someone or some situation, we don't have to figure out God's will in advance. Nor do we have to use any words. We can just claim the wonderful promise that when we are at our wit's end in a situation and don't know how to pray, that the Spirit within will intercede on our behalf. And wonder of wonders, since the Spirit always prays through us according to the will of God, the prayer will always be answered. Our part is merely to sense the need and humbly come to Him in faith, knowing that we do not know how to pray.

Marge and I have a prayer practice which we frequently use when we pray for our "23"—our five children, their spouses, and our thirteen grandchildren. We take turns mentioning one of the 23, and in our mind's eye we lift that child or grandchild up to the Lord. Our attitude is, "Thy will be done," but we refrain from analyzing any current "need" and we ask for nothing. We have come to realize that we don't know how to pray, so by faith we just trust that the all-knowing Spirit of Love will intercede for the one on whom we are focused.

In *The Cloud of Unknowing*, an anonymous prayer classic written in 14th-century England, the author teaches about "contemplation," the historic prayer practice in which we respond to God's call to "Be still and know that I am God." That prayer of the heart is our acknowledgment of the reality of our inner spiritual union, of the mystery of the Gospel, and of the Absolute Other who is beyond words, images and sight.

Instead of all our self-conscious and self-centered efforts to be "good" and to learn more *about* God, we should learn *just to be with Him* and allow ourselves the luxury of being loved and possessed by Him. It's in the faith practice of contemplation, or centering prayer, that we will enter into the mystery of God's presence within—into the cloud of unknowing. We will have moved from taking from the deadly tree of *knowing* to the Life found in the Tree of *Unknowing*.

Mature life in the Spirit is more than "cause and effect." It's more than increasing our knowledge *about* God and life. It's meant to be a spiritual journey from knowing to unknowing—from being know-it-all's to becoming poor in spirit. Life is an on-going growth process in our awareness of the divine mystery—the mystery that it is no longer we who live, but Christ who lives in us.

12

DISCOVERING OUR DESTINY IN ADVERSITY

At times God puts us through the discipline of darkness to teach us to heed Him. Song birds are taught to sing in the dark, and we are put into the shadow of God's hand until we learn to hear Him. "What I tell you in darkness"—watch where God puts you in darkness, and when you are there keep your mouth shut.

Are you in the dark just now in your circumstances, or in your life with God? Then remain quiet. If you open your mouth in the dark, you will talk in the wrong mood: darkness is the time to listen. Don't talk to other people about it; don't read books to find out the reason for the darkness, but listen and heed. If you talk to other people, you cannot hear what God is saying. When you are in the dark, listen, and God will give you a very precious message for someone else when you get into the light.

After every time of darkness there comes a mixture of delight and humiliation (if there is delight only, I question whether we have heard God at all). Delight in hearing God speak, but chiefly delight in humiliation. What a long time I was in hearing that! How slow I have been in understanding that! And yet God has been saying it all these days and weeks. Now He gives you the gift of humiliation which brings the softness of heart that will always listen to God now.

—*Oswald Chambers*

12

DISCOVERING OUR DESTINY IN ADVERSITY

On June 2, 1995, U.S. Air Force Captain Scott O'Grady's F-16 was shot down by a missile over Bosnia. For the next six days countless concerned Americans, myself included, closely followed the intense media coverage and the heart-wrenching family interviews, when no one knew for certain whether Scott O'Grady was dead or alive. Rumor and speculation abounded.

When O'Grady was rescued by a contingent of sixty-one Marines in four helicopters—backed up by another forty aircraft and many more troops—we all breathed a huge sigh of relief. Over the next few days we were amazed to hear the details of O'Grady's raw courage and deep faith in the midst of seemingly hopeless adversity. Ejecting from his F-16 at 26,000 feet, he parachuted into an area infested with hostile soldiers and civilians. Enemy search parties came within five feet of his hiding place. His only food for six days was a little grass and a few ants.

In the last chapter of his book, *Return With Honor*, O'Grady summarizes his ordeal as follows:

> *Those six days in Bosnia were a religious retreat for me, a total spiritual renewal. I'm not recommending*

*near-death experience for its own sake; it's a ride I
wouldn't care to take again. But I will say that my time
in Bosnia was completely positive—nothing bad has
come out of it. From the instant that my plane blew up
around me, and I opened my heart to God's love, I felt
the most incredible freedom—my joy was unbounded.
That day, five miles up, with death at my front door, I
found the key to life. It took a big jolt to open my eyes,
but it was worth it; I knew I'd never be lost again.*

How would we have responded if we were in
O'Grady's place? Would we have labelled such an
experience "a spiritual retreat, a total spiritual renewal"?
What was the source of O'Grady's incredible response to
such an impossible situation?

In all the interviews after his rescue, as well as
throughout his book, O'Grady unashamedly credits his
"faith in God, the Source of all goodness," and the prayers
and love of his family and friends, as the reason he made
it back against overwhelming odds. He made it back
because he had the uncanny ability to see a loving God
operating in the midst of the most negative circumstances.
By faith, he opened his heart to God's love in the face of
utter darkness. He saw as "good" what most people
would label as "horrible." He had discovered his destiny—
an awareness of God's loving presence—during the
greatest adversity of his life.

In my opinion, *Time* magazine missed it in their choice
of Person of the Year for 1995. My vote would have been
for Scott O'Grady, an example of courage and faith for
other Americans and for people everywhere!

Adversity brings us face to face with who we really
are. It forces us to find out whether our life is based on
faith or mere lip-service to a philosophy.

A couple of years ago my wife Marge and I went to her
50-year high school class reunion. About 250 of her

classmates (out of a graduating class of 720) met for an evening to get reacquainted and exchange stories. I, along with all the other spouses and escorts, dutifully stood by listening and observing, politely entering into the various interchanges whenever possible.

What an eye-opener! 500 people—most of whom were 67 or 68 years old—milling around before the banquet, trying to recapture in a few words some of the past, as well as share some of the meaningful experiences of the intervening fifty years. It was a grand mixture of stories of blessings and curses, of joys and sorrows, of dreams fulfilled and dreams shattered.

Yes, for me, it was "a grand mixture of blessings and curses." Though it could have been depressing to hear about all the classmates and friends who had divorced, or contracted cancer or AIDS, or lost their jobs, or died (about half of Marge's classmates are dead or unaccounted for), the experience made me think about the source and reason for adversity. I saw in all the adversity the opportunity for adventure; I saw through the negatives to my Father who is All and in all.

I had been prepared for this reunion by a sermon from our pastor the previous week. He had used Matthew 10:29-31 as his sermon text: "Not a sparrow will fall to the ground apart from your Father. Therefore do not fear: you are of more value than many sparrows." The words "apart from your Father" turned on a light in my being that has substantially changed my outlook on adversity. In the past I had always tended to forget that I am not alone, that God is in charge, and that nothing could separate me from His love for even one minute. So I would try handling the trouble on my own, relying on my own strength and ability.

Though the focus of the pastor's message was that God loves us and will take care of us, what I heard was that apart from my Father, nothing good or evil can touch me, or anyone else. All agents and agencies of evil (and good) must work through the one Principal (God) of the universe. This means that in its essence life is not random, willy-nilly, or out-of-control. God is not dead. God is very much involved in every circumstance of life, be it good or evil.

No story in the Bible illustrates this more clearly than the timeless story of Job. It clearly proves to me that this is a one-Power, not a two-power, universe. Satan, God's convenient agent, seems to talk God into testing Job, but it is clear that it is God who prescribes the limits of the tests.

Was it God or was it Satan who was responsible for Job's troubles? Was this an illustration of the "permissive will of God," or was this the "determined will of God"? Satan clearly acknowledges God's direct involvement when he says the same thing to God in both tests: "Put forth *Thy* hand" (1:11 and 2:5). Satan knew it was God who was in control! Whether or not we understand it or agree with it, God was directly involved in Job's adversity. We don't need to protect God's reputation by talking about the "permissive will of God."

Yes, our loving heavenly Father is involved in both our blessings and our curses. The ultimate proof text for me on God's total sovereignty is Isaiah 45:7—"I am the Lord...the One forming light and creating darkness, causing well-being and *creating calamity*." Obviously, God is not reticent to use adversity, if that is what is necessary, to bring His precious children to discover their true destiny in Christ.

Let's look at Job's experience. Though Job was the most righteous person on earth, he didn't really *know* God. In his darkest hour—engulfed by unbelievable tragedy—life-changing enlightenment finally came. Job needed to be stripped of all his self-righteousness, so that he could be brought to faith, trust and the knowledge of God.

As long as blessings were being poured out on Job for his righteousness, his faith in God was sure. He could believe what he had heard about God. But Job had to learn to trust God in everything, in adversity as well as in times of blessing. He had heard *about* God, but he still needed to see Him for who He really is. Job needed to see his own smallness, pettiness and self-righteousness in contrast to the true greatness of the one and only Principal of the universe. Job had to see that apart from God's loving mercy he was a dead man.

We will only experience "the patience of Job" when we discover what he discovered: that nothing—not even our self-centeredness and our blindness—can separate us from the presence and love of God. It's that awareness, and the repentance that comes with it, that reveals to us our destiny in Christ. Like Job, we need to sit patiently and wait on God at all times, even during times of adversity. Then we will discover that God has not abandoned us, but rather, that He is nearer than we ever believed possible.

There are few promises sweeter than an obscure passage in Isaiah 30:20-21 *(RSV):*

> *And though the Lord give you the bread of adversity and the water of affliction, yet your Teacher will not hide Himself any more, but your eyes shall see your Teacher. And your ears shall hear a word behind you saying, "This is the way, walk in it," when you turn to the right or when you turn to the left.*

It is in times of adversity, discipline and pressure that our eyes are opened to Reality, to God Himself, to God's unfailing presence. If you want to see and hear God, and experience His intimacy and involvement in all things, then you can expect troubles to come along as part of the package. But it's worth it. The verses that follow the above passage promise blessings to "all those who wait on Him."

The story of Joseph is another classic example of someone who discovered his destiny in the midst of unbelievable adversity. After all the things that happened to him, the depth of Joseph's understanding of God is captured in his startling comment to the brothers who had sold him into slavery: "You meant evil against me, but God meant it for good in order to bring about this present result."

Joseph saw through his negative circumstances. He knew God in a way that many of us don't. He knew the God of whom David spoke when he said, "Even the darkness is not dark to You...darkness and light are alike to You" (Ps.139:12). God intends that we see Him in *all* things—not just in blessings. He is ever present and at work, whether the situation is good or evil. Though we might define evil as that which is destructive and negative, when it is seen through the single eye of faith—through the prism of God's purpose and infinite love—we will only see His goodness and grace.

When I was in the military during World War II, I had contact with the Christian group called "Navigators." One of their emphases was the importance of Scripture memorization. The first verse they recommended was I Corinthians 10:13—"No temptation has overtaken you but such as is common to man; and God is faithful, who will not allow you to be tempted beyond what you are able; but with the temptation will provide the way of escape also, that you may be able to endure it."

It's a verse that was hard for me to memorize, but which I have never forgotten. Let's face it, temptation gets our attention. It's God's clever way to press each of us into choosing His "way of escape." It's a built-in "calling card" from our Lover, to remind us that we are not alone and that we cannot make it on our own. We need Him and His grace or we will surely mess up.

God's plan for us from the beginning was that we be tempted. He knew that temptations would cause us to look beyond ourselves for His answer, for His way of escape.

Being created in God's image, we were given freedom of choice. When God created Adam and Eve, He said, "From any tree of the garden you may freely eat; but from the tree of the knowledge of good and evil you shall not eat." With this pronouncement came choice—and tension. Tension has been woven ever since into every thread of the fabric of life. The tensions of life are basic to bringing us to salvation, as well as in bringing us to our destiny as "extensions of The Incarnation." Tensions are used by God to cause us to turn to Him, our "way of escape."

We are all subjected, directly or indirectly, to an endless string of life's tensions: crippling diseases and accidents, financial reverses, dark nights of the soul, family misunderstandings, marital discord, untimely death, inordinate affections, unwanted habits, etc. These things are common to all. Even Jesus was tempted—"tempted in all things as we are, yet without sin" (Heb.4:15). What was Jesus' way of escape? To turn His eyes away from the temptation and to look to His Father. What is our way of escape? To turn our eyes away from the temptation and to look to God.

Remember, the first thing to see is that the tension— the adversity, the dilemma, the circumstance, the weakness—is not our problem. The problem is in our reaction, it's in our seeing and in our choosing. The truth is that the tension is a blessing in disguise—it's our springboard to faith. For the tension is what forces us to humbly acknowledge our helplessness and to turn to God in faith, instead of relying on our own strength and ability.

In the next chapter we will see that as we discover our destiny in the tensions and adversities of life, life becomes amazingly simple.

13

IT'S ALL
VERY SIMPLE

"**A**sk and you shall receive." The prayer of the faithful is infinitely powerful because it harnesses all the power of the Infinite. But the God of love does not listen to the lispings of human lips. He hears only the beating of human hearts and what rests within them.

It is the compassion that comes out of the experience of oneness and holds the world in infinitely tender love that speaks efficaciously to the Divine Creative Love and alters the course of history. It is not some beautiful thought or insightful idea, but being with the groanings of the earth and all its peoples that makes our prayer.

It is not ideas that are going to make us effective cosmic persons able to make a difference in the redeeming of the earth: it is only our living out of the Center of unity and oneness.

—*M. Basil Pennington*

13

IT'S ALL
VERY SIMPLE

Words, words, words! How many times have you picked up a Christian book or magazine (including *Union Life*), read a while, and then said to yourself, "Why do they use so many words? Why do they have to make it so difficult? Why can't it be simpler?"

It *can* be simpler. Life, the meaning of life, and even our Christian faith shouldn't be as hard to understand and elusive as we all make it. Since not everyone is a theologian, a psychologist, a professor or a rocket scientist, why doesn't someone explain all this stuff in a way that is simple, so it can be used in everyday life?

It just so happens that Someone already has! God spells it all out very simply and clearly in a few verses in Deuteronomy 30, and then underscores it in a follow-up passage in the New Testament in Romans 10. In the Old Testament passage, God sums it all up when He says, "So choose life in order that you may live...by loving the Lord your God, by obeying His voice, and by holding fast to Him." In effect, God is saying, "Just focus on your love relationship with Me and you will have found the meaning of life. Then you can live life to the full."

This simple command from God (through Moses) was given to the children of Israel after their forty years of wandering in the wilderness. The time had come to enter the Promised Land and to enjoy the inheritance that God had planned for them.

But before giving the Israelites the simple formula of, "Love God and you will live," God first laid down the Law in detail. The first 29 chapters of Deuteronomy contain literally hundreds of commandments—along with the blessings and curses that would result from obedience and disobedience. After hearing the details of the Law, the Israelites were ready to throw up their hands and shout, "That's impossible!"

And that is exactly what God wanted them (and us) to understand. God's answer to their reaction of "That's impossible!" was, in effect, "You're right!"

In Chapter 30, He meets them at their point of need and gives them the promise of the wherewithal for a love relationship with God—a changed heart: "The Lord your God will circumcise your heart...to love the Lord your God" (v.6).

God promises us the gift of a changed heart so that we too, by faith, can choose to love Him and live. "For," He continues, "this commandment [to love] which I command you this day is not too difficult for you, nor is it out of reach....The word is very near you, in your mouth and in your heart, that you may observe it."

Yes, the answer is very simple and very close to us. We don't have to go up to the heavens or cross the sea to get what we need. The Kingdom and the Power is already within us. God told the Israelites in the wilderness, and He tells us the same thing through Paul today: "The word is very near you, in your mouth and in your heart."

These verses provide an interesting play on the word "word." God's commandment to love is His *written* word to us. Our response is the *spoken* word in our mouth, our verbalized word of faith. And the indwelling spirit of Christ is the *living* Word in our hearts.

The point to remember is that God is always the Initiator and we are always responders. He gives the word (the command), He prompts our word (the response), and His Spirit is the word within (the power to obey).

Just before graduating from high school, I enlisted in the aviation branch of the U.S. Navy. It was 1943, and the United States was deeply involved in World War II, both in Europe and in the Pacific. The decision was easy, as I had only two alternatives: enlist in the Service branch of my choice, or be drafted as a buck private in the Army. I chose Naval Aviation.

One day after my eighteenth birthday I was officially inducted into the Navy. That June morning marked the beginning of over four years in the military. My first orders took me to a small college in Newberry, South Carolina, for pre-flight schooling. After an all-night train ride from Chicago, I found myself at the Administration Building, in the first of many long lines, waiting to receive my room assignment, uniforms, etc.

Though a half-century has gone by, and many events have faded from my memory, or been completely forgotten, one detail of my first day in Service is as clear as if it happened yesterday. Shortly after going to my room and meeting the three recruits who would be my roommates for the next year, a loudspeaker blared in the hall outside our door: "Now hear this! Now hear this! This is the word! All trainees are to report on the double to...."

I remember this detail vividly, because during the next year that same loudspeaker blared out those same words hundreds of times: "Now hear this! Now hear this! This is the word"—followed by the instructions we were to obey. The voice had no body that I could identify, but it was always there, always giving us "the word" about something.

In a similar way God, likewise without a readily identifiable body, is forever giving us "the word," and that word is life-changing. In reality, "the word" is already in us; it's in every Christian. It is the "ultimate word" which Paul speaks of in Romans 10:8: "The word is near you, in your mouth and in your heart—that is, *the word of faith* which we are preaching." When we truly understand the power and significance of this ultimate word—the word of faith, acknowledging in words what we believe in our hearts—we will be well on our way to handling all the riddles of life and the universe. We will not necessarily know all the answers, but we will be much more content to live by faith, knowing that all things work together for the good of those who love God.

I closed my first book, *The Wink of Faith*, with Paul's universal call to recognize that the living Word (Jesus Christ) dwells in the hearts of all who are believers: "Test yourselves to see if you are in the faith; examine yourselves! Or do you not recognize this about yourselves, that Jesus Christ is in you—unless indeed you fail the test?" (II Cor. 13:5.)

Have you tested yourself to see if you are in the faith? Do you recognize that Jesus Christ is indeed in you, and that He is your very life? Do you know that because of your union with Him you are a new creature and a partaker of His divine nature? Are you convinced that the Kingdom of God is within you? Are you comfortable in saying that you are an expression of Christ with whom you are united as one?

If you can answer yes to these questions, then you are ready to embrace Paul's all-important words: "The word is near you, in your mouth and in your heart, that is, *the word of faith*." I believe it's no exaggeration to say that these four words summarize the heart of Paul's message. For it is by the word of faith that all Christians are meant to live out their lives.

In a limited but very real sense, all our words, positive and negative, are words of faith. Whatever we believe and say becomes our reality. If our believing is positive, it's labeled "faith"; if negative, it's labeled "unbelief." Although you might have tremendous talent, if you are convinced that you will fail, and keep saying so, you undoubtedly will. Our beliefs dictate our experience.

When we disbelieved in God, then for us He did not exist; we led godless and miserable lives. When we believed in Christ, nothing about God changed; He had always loved us. But we changed dramatically into new creatures, because our believing changed. Whatever words we speak from a heart conviction sooner or later give birth to life-changing results, for better or for worse.

Notice the passage that follows my "ultimate word" ("the word is very near you") verse : "That if you confess with your mouth Jesus as Lord, and believe in your heart that God raised Him from the dead, you shall be saved; for with the heart a person believes, resulting in righteousness, and with the mouth he confesses, resulting in salvation" (Rom. 10:9-10).

Except for John 3:16, no other passage of Scripture has been more instrumental in leading unbelievers to Christ. For these words of Paul clearly state the two facets of salvation: (1) a heart belief and (2) a confession with the mouth. We need the Word within and a word without. We must experience an inner revelation by the Spirit of Christ (the living Word) before we can make an outer expression, or confession, of our persuasion.

Every "word of faith" contains these two elements: an inner revelation and an outer expression. These were the ingredients of our first word of faith when we were born again, and exactly the same ingredients enable us to be whole persons and live fulfilled lives, as we move from false self to true self.

How does the "ultimate word" work? Can it be simply a matter of speaking a few words of faith? Yes! Was there anything complicated about our conversion? Of course not. It was a simple response to a heart knowing. Granted, our search for Life may have included years of preparation that were difficult and onerous, but when the light finally went on, we simply acknowledged what we inwardly believed. We recognized ourselves as God's children.

The working out of our Christian life is meant to be just as simple, even though we might not think so during our second great search. The first forty-one years of my life as a Christian were spent in a wilderness searching for meaningful answers to the perplexing questions of life. When I finally knew something of who I really am in Christ, and saw the glory of my destiny as a co-heir with Him, the fulfilling life I had been striving for became much simpler. In truth, it has always been there! God was telling me the same thing He told the children of Israel.

Paul's words in Romans 10:8 are a direct quote from Deuteronomy 30. He summed them up in a new expression—the word of faith—but there was nothing new about the simplicity and availability of the word in our mouths and hearts. The mystery of the inner Word—Christ in us, the hope of glory—was substantially hidden until the revelation of Jesus Christ, but the truth has always been simple and available for those who see through the eyes of faith.

It is this all-inclusive word of faith that I want to continue to emphasize and share. It includes both the soul's outer word of faith (the human "Yes!") and the Holy Spirit's inner word of faith (the divine "Yes!"). Ultimately, eternal life is these two words becoming one. The word in our mouth becomes one with the word in our heart; outer and Inner become one. Our free will becomes one with the sovereign will of God.

Any attempt to capture faith and the mystery of the indwelling Christ and put it into words is bound to have some serious limitations. *So I urge you to let go of all the words, and to come to Christ daily in silence.* Allow His faith to replace yours. Allow His light to dispel your darkness. Trust the Teacher within you to answer your questions. As His divine therapy heals you of your wounds, and His unconditional love transforms you, you will see that loving yourself, loving Him and loving the world around you is not "too difficult or out of reach"—it is not impossible after all.

Yes, life really is very simple. For us, as for the Israelites back in the time of Moses, the Law is reduced to a single, simple commandment—love God and love your neighbor as yourself. It's simple because the wherewithal that we need to keep this commandment is already within us. It's not out of reach. The Kingdom of God is within. Christ in us, the hope of glory, is one with us.

As we see the reality of our union with Christ, by faith we will begin to know and experience God's love—for God is love. As we allow our love relationship with the Trinity to transform us, the Lover dwelling in our hearts will gradually confer on us the fruit of the Spirit—everything from love, joy and peace to self-control. And at last we will be ready to live in the preciousness of the present moment.

14

THE PRECIOUSNESS
OF THE
PRESENT MOMENT

The present moment holds infinite riches beyond your wildest dreams, but you will only enjoy them to the extent of your faith and love. The more a soul loves, the more it longs; the more it hopes, the more it finds. The will of God is manifest in each moment, an immense ocean which the heart only fathoms in so far as it overflows with faith, trust and love.

To discover God in the smallest and most ordinary things, as well as in the greatest, is to possess a rare and sublime faith. To find contentment in the present moment is to relish and adore the divine will in the succession of all the things to be done and suffered which make up the duty to the present moment.

—*Jean Pierre de Caussade*

14

THE PRECIOUSNESS
OF THE
PRESENT MOMENT

In the Fall of 1995, Marge and I attended our first silent two-day contemplative-prayer retreat. About 80 of us spent a weekend together at the Warrenville Cenacle, a local convent.

Our speaker was James Finley. As a young man, Finley spent six years at the Abbey of Gethsemani, a Trappist monastery in Kentucky, with Thomas Merton as his mentor. Finley presently practices psychotherapy in California, in addition to leading over twenty contemplative-prayer retreats each year.

There were five teaching sessions by Finley, over the course of the weekend, with the balance of the time spent in virtual silence. Early in the first session, Finley made a statement that will serve as the basis for this closing chapter. It went like this: "Life is the awareness of the preciousness of the immediacy of the present moment." The first time he rattled off this mouthful of words, I whispered to Marge: "What did he just say? Did you write that down? That's important!"

Marge's response was, "Sssh!"

Fortunately, Finley repeated the statement in that session and in later ones. Interestingly, I don't think he ever explained it in detail or elaborated on it in any way. He apparently thought it was self-explanatory. But I must confess that the first couple of times I heard him say, "Life is the awareness of the preciousness of the immediacy of the present moment," it sounded like double-talk.

Though parts of the statement kept passing through my mind, I had trouble remembering the sequence of the three prepositional phrases. So I finally wrote it out on the back of one of my business cards, which I then put in my billfold for quick reference. During the sessions I kept pulling it out and re-reading it.

During one of the scheduled meditation times for that day, Marge and I were walking alongside the creek that runs through the retreat property. Our daughter-in-law, Claudia, was sitting by the water's edge reading a book she had just borrowed from the Cenacle library. It was an English translation of Jean-Pierre de Caussade's eighteenth-century French classic, *The Sacrament of the Present Moment.*

It intrigued me that the title of the book was reminiscent of Finley's words. So I convinced (pressured!) Claudia to let me borrow it right then and there. Before the next session I had read most of the book. So when Finley repeated his statement, I was better able to understand its importance.

However, it wasn't until weeks later that I appreciated the fuller significance of each phrase. I had no trouble in understanding the import of "awareness" and "preciousness" and "the present moment," but where did "immediacy" fit in? When I looked it up in the dictionary, I found that the primary definitions were: "the state or quality of being immediate; freedom from the intervention of any person or thing; direct relation or connection." "Immediate" means "no intervening member." In other words, Finley's statement means "the right-here-and-now-ness of the present moment." Interestingly, one of the definitions of "immediacy" when used in the area of philosophy is "intuitive knowledge as distinguished from that arrived at by proof or reasoning."

In any event, I concluded that it probably would not be wrong to substitute the word "oneness" for the word "immediacy" in the quotation. It could just as well read: "Life is the awareness of the preciousness of the *oneness* of the present moment."

I realized that it is only when life is seen in the context of "immediacy"—that is, in the light of our inseparable union with Christ, of our *oneness* with God—that each person and each situation can be seen as precious. For it is our awareness of God's presence with us—His immediacy—in each situation that changes our outlook as well as our actions. Only then do we see the preciousness of every second we are alive, as well as the infinite possibilities of each moment.

But living from the inside out—with an awareness of the immediacy, the closeness of God's presence—seems so elusive, doesn't it? Living as we always have, with outward things uppermost in our minds, seems so much more comfortable and safe.

This reminds me of the six-year-old girl who ran into her parents' bedroom during a violent thunderstorm. After they had comforted her, the father carried her back to her bedroom. As he was about to leave, he said, "Don't worry, sweetheart, God will be here with you when I leave." To which the little girl responded, "Daddy, if you don't mind, why don't you stay here with God; I'm going back to sleep with Mommy!" It always seems easier and safer to live in our feelings than it does to live by faith.

Until we know, beyond a shadow of doubt, that "nothing can separate us from the love of God"—until we see every moment as a precious new adventure to explore and enjoy—we will be missing out on life. Yes, "Life is *awareness*"—and our awareness of the preciousness of God and the present moment can be

139

expanded by simply doing as the Psalm says: *Be still and know that I am God.*

As we take this step of faith, God gifts us with a new seeing of His immediacy in every event in life—be it sweet or sour. We come to see that the intervention of any person or thing in our lives is God-ordained, no matter how it looks. We see that God has a hedge around us as surely as He had one around Job. We see that as "not one sparrow falls to the ground apart from the Father," so there is nothing that happens to us that God doesn't know about and ordain! Finally we are able to label all things as "good" and see all things as "precious."

Is there a special significance to the term *"present moment"*? Yes, to God there is only *now*, only an eternal present moment. God is not subject to time—to the past or to the future. He knows only "isness." He knows only present moments as a continuum, as the eternal now— not as part of "time." Remember what God calls Himself? *"I Am."*

So, what about past moments and future moments? God lives in the eternal moment where there is no past or future. Only we are caught up with the past and the future. But the more we see that our "life is hid with Him in heavenly places," the more we, too, will live in the present moment. There we will experience heaven, where "time shall be no longer" (Rev. 10:6 *KJV*). But the freedom that comes from the experience of timelessness is reserved for those who stop trying to relive the past or control the future—for those who see past and future as illusions compared to the true reality of the eternal now.

When we focus on the past—with either pride or regret, depending upon our analysis of the cause and effect of each situation—our favorite phrase is, "If only...." *If only such and such had or hadn't happened.* The fact is that nothing happens "apart from the Father." That is why Paul said,

"...sorrow that is according to the will of God produces a repentance without regret" (II Cor. 7:10). In the wisdom of hindsight, we purpose to change direction, but we aren't meant to live in regret.

On the other hand, it is just as foolish to live in the future, yearning and grasping for a change of circumstances. For if we focus on the future, we live in a "never-never land" of endless goals, worries and expectations, always waiting for the big break—once again missing the preciousness of the present moment. Like a broken record, we will continue to say, "Things will be different when...." But we can't enjoy the present if we continue to focus on the future.

Even if the "big break" comes, we will not be satisfied. For the simple truth is that nothing changes until we learn to see things differently, until we learn to see from God's perspective: that Christ is All and in all. We will only see and experience the preciousness of the present moment to the extent that we see the immediacy—the presence—of Christ in every person and every circumstance. Is this possible? Will we ever be able to say with Paul, "I have learned to be content in whatever circumstance I am in"?

For me, there is no passage in Scripture more challenging than Philippians 4:11-13. Not only does Paul claim that he has learned total contentment in every circumstance, but he goes on to say, "I have learned the secret of being filled and going hungry, both of having abundance and suffering need." In other words, he has learned the secret of *being*—whatever the circumstances. And he caps off the passage with the audacious assertion, "I can do all things through Him who strengthens me."

That's what I call "abundant living," and being "more than conquerors"! Will we ever learn to experience "the secret of being" Paul talks about? The answer lies in recognizing and experiencing "the glory of this mystery [secret]...which is Christ in you, the hope of glory" (Col. 1:27). The liberating secret of *being* is only available to us to the extent that we realize our inner Divine union with the Beloved. The secret of being is in seeing Christ as our Spouse; it's in being in love with God.

Was there ever a time in your life when everything seemed to be just perfect? How about when you first experienced puppy love, or an extreme infatuation, or an all-encompassing love? At that point, being in love and being with your beloved was all that mattered. You were anxious about nothing, for your mutual love was everything. You both felt invincible, your dreams had no boundaries, and you knew only the preciousness of the rapturous moment. In the same way, we will find that the secret to life, the secret of being, is simply being in love with God; it is being captured and raptured by God's love, and simultaneously responding in kind.

That is what life is all about: responding to our Lover's overtures of unconditional love. The Hound of Heaven has never ceased to chase us and solicit our intimacy and love. But we need to allow ourselves to be so taken by His great love that we can do nothing but love Him with all our heart, mind and soul.

Though many of us give lip-service to the truth that we are the bride of Christ, most of us have been reluctant brides. For one thing, there is a big difference between believing that we, as a small part of a large Church, are the bride of Christ, and in believing that Christ has called us to one-on-one intimacy as His bride. We feel much safer as an unidentified part of a large group, where the relationship is less personal, less intimate and less scary. Just as our salvation is individual, our union relationship with Christ is meant to be personal and intimate.

God longs for us to see that we are not separated from Him. Ever since the tearing of the temple veil at the time of the death of our Lord, God's *immediacy* has been available to us. At the precise moment that Jesus cried out, yielded up His spirit and died on the Cross, "...the veil of the temple was torn in two from top to bottom..." (Matt. 27:51). In the drama of all that happened at the time of the death and resurrection of Jesus, it is easy to overlook this important event. For this tearing from top to bottom of the veil in the temple meant that God would no longer keep Himself separated from His people. Shortly thereafter, on the day of Pentecost, Divine Presence would have a new dwelling place: the individual hearts of His people. God would have a new home in the heart of each believer.

For a number of centuries the *Shekinah*—the dwelling place of the visible presence of God—was in the "Most Holy Place," in the "heart" of the Jewish temple. The "presence" was only visible as a pillar of cloud or fire above the ark of the covenant. A heavy piece of tapestry separated the larger center section of the temple—called the Holy Place—from the Most Holy Place, into which the high priest went once a year to offer sacrifice for the sins of the people. But all that is history.

Since the once-and-for-all sacrifice of the Great High Priest, the temple made with hands is no longer the dwelling place of God. Now, the dwelling place of God— the "Most Holy Place"—is in human hearts. Humanity no longer has to approach God through an intermediary; no longer is there any separation between us and God. "The mystery which has been hidden...has now been manifested to His saints" (Col. 1:27).

How is it, then, that so many of us still continue to live in fear, condemnation and separation? It's because we don't *see* God—we don't recognize the magnitude of His love, forgiveness and power.

In II Corinthians 3:15-16, Paul reminds us that a veil (false self) lies over our hearts until we "turn to the Lord" and "the veil is taken away." We have a part in the gradual removal of that many-layered veil (a veil of separation caused by our blindness to the magnitude of false self). The layers of that veil are the result of many wounds, many misconceptions and much darkness. Our part is to turn to the Lord. We must respond to our Lover's call; we must look to Jesus, the author and perfecter of our faith.

One of my favorite hymns says it all:

Turn your eyes upon Jesus,
Look full in His wonderful face,
And the things of earth will grow strangely dim
In the light of His glory and grace.

Peter's experience when he stepped out of the boat and walked on water is a wonderful illustration of the importance of keeping our eyes on Christ, of having an awareness of our Lord at all times. As Jesus beckoned Peter to come to Him, Peter fixed his eyes on Jesus and miraculously started to walk on the water. It was only as Peter was distracted, suddenly becoming aware of himself, that he took his eyes off Jesus, and began to sink.

The promise in II Corinthians 3:18 of our transformation into the image of Christ is to all who with "unveiled face" behold "as in a mirror the glory of the Lord." We must choose to respond to God's loving call and turn to Christ, our Lover, with whom we are in union. As we acknowledge His presence within, as well as His transcendent glory, we closet ourselves away in intimate communion with our Spouse, yielding ourselves in silence to God's glorious love. A metamorphosis begins to take place. We are transformed into His likeness and, like Moses, we spontaneously reflect His glory to our local world.

One of the wonderful by-products of centering prayer, according to James Finley, is the "tendency of the heart and mind to gravitate toward the center of the present moment, where God holds us in His embrace.... Right in the midst of one's daily work there is given, at times, momentary flashes of the divine dimension of the task at hand."

As we are faithful to our centering prayer practice, we will start to see and experience life differently—with less fear, less judgment, less tenseness; and with a lot more wonder, more playfulness, and more tender affection. A measure of this transformation will stealthily become evident to us and to others. As God heals us and fills us with His love, we, too, will begin to experience "momentary flashes of the divine dimension," times of *spontaneous centered living*. My own recent experience has evidenced this again and again in small, but significant, ways. Here are a few random illustrations.

One of the first major changes was that I learned how to smile again. Like Martha of Bethany, I took my Christian life very seriously. My face reflected a perpetual anxiety— I virtually did not know how to smile. My extreme, eager self-effort had resulted in a debilitating self-consciousness. I could not look anyone in the eye, and any attempt to smile was artificial. When it was photo time for the family, I always insisted on taking the pictures. I felt like an ugly duckling, and any attempt to smile froze on my face. But now I can smile again, inside and out; I can look into anyone's eyes—and it's wonderful! I know God's merciful, healing hand has restored some of my childhood innocence.

A new, spontaneous gratitude is another wonderful gift that God has given me over the past couple of years. Daily, in the midst of my busy schedule, any number of "meaningful coincidences" arise which convince me that God is totally involved in the details of my life. He reminds me to place an important telephone call. He leads me to a misplaced file that I had not been able to find. He whispers an insightful word that enables me to minimize a thorny employee situation, or more efficiently handle an accounting or other business problem.

The gift of an awareness of His intervention in my day-to-day life is special, but it is equally wonderful for me to experience the gift of a spontaneous surge of gratitude. An "Oh, thank you, thank you, Lord" response wells up from within, again and again. And, at the same time, my new smile registers without and within.

Yet another sign of inner transformation is a new attentiveness to the presence of my wife, my family and my business associates. I catch myself *being* with "precious persons," instead of always trying to *fix* everyone, getting them to listen to me, or trying to change them to embrace my opinions and my outlook. In conversations, I find myself interrupting others less and listening more—giving the other person the courtesy of my attention, instead of planning my next major pronouncement!

So I am finding, in innumerable ways, that "those who wait on the Lord will not be disappointed." Gradually, ever so gradually, the discipline of our periodic faith-practice of the prayer of silence results in a *transforming union* and a *contemplative life*.

The practice of basking in the presence of our Lover eventually results in responses that reflect the full spectrum of the fruit of the Spirit. The love, joy, and peace for which our hearts have always yearned gradually becomes a reality in our lives. Out of us will flow rivers of living water to our world.

We will have found the pearl of great price: a glorious Person who adores us and is one with us. He comes to us with the ultimate gift: experiential love. As we bask in the warmth of this gift, our icy hearts are thawed and we are empowered to go out and give freely the love we have received. We go out to love the world.

EPILOGUE

Often we will do much more to make men and women contemplatives by leaving them alone and minding our own business—which is contemplation itself—than by breaking in on them with what we think we know about the interior life.

For when we are united with God in silence and darkness and when our faculties are raised above the level of their own natural activity, and rest in the pure, tranquil, incomprehensible cloud that surrounds the presence of God, our prayer and the grace that is given to us tend of their very nature to overflow invisibly through the Mystical Body of Christ. We who dwell together invisibly in the bond of the One Spirit of God affect one another more than we can ever realize by our own union with God, by our spiritual vitality in Him.

Therefore, the best way to prepare ourselves for the possible vocation of sharing contemplation with others is not to study how to talk and reason about contemplation, but to withdraw ourselves as much as we can from talk and argument, and return into the silence and humility of heart in which God will purify our love of all of its human imperfections.

Then in His own time, He will set our hand to the work He wants us to do, and we will find ourselves doing it without being quite able to realize how we got there, or how it all got started.

—*Thomas Merton*

EPILOGUE

*B*asking *In His Presence* is my call to the Church to return to the prayer of silence. It's a call to contemplative prayer; a call to centering prayer; a call to behold Christ within; a call to practice His presence; a call to be still; a call to wordless prayer; a call to experience Christ praying through us; a call to a tryst with our Lover.

One of the most well-known and loved hymns of the Church is "In the Garden." I frequently preface my times of basking in His presence with these personalized words from that song:

> *And You walk with me,*
> *And You talk with me,*
> *And You tell me I am Your own,*
> *And the joy we share,*
> *As we tarry there,*
> *None other has ever known.*

And as I have practiced the prayer of silence, this has been my experience—incomparable joy, joy unspeakable.

Lovers through the ages are convinced that their love is an incomparable love. They have written and sung about that love. Most of us have experienced a love affair which is amazingly sweet and which we felt was unique. Alas, these "loves" rarely last.

But there is a lasting love affair available to all.

I am convinced that if you have a tryst with your indwelling Lover a couple of times each day, you will experience a love affair that will never end. It will get sweeter every day. And it will gradually transform you into a person who is like Christ—gentle and humble in heart. You will have found your Soul-mate, the One for whom your heart has always longed.

CREDITS

(for quotes preceding each chapter)

Page 16. Taken from UNION WITH GOD by Jeanne Guyon, © Copyright 1981 by Gene Edwards. Published by Christian Books, Augusta, Maine.

Page 26. Taken from A TREE FULL OF ANGELS by Macrina Wiederkehr, © Copyright 1988 Harper & Row, Inc. Published by Harper & Row, San Francisco, California.

Page 36. Taken from THE SPIRITUAL GUIDE by Michael Molinos, © Copyright 1982 by Christian Books. Published by The Seedsowers, Christian Books Publishing House, Sargent, Georgia.

Page 44. Taken from THE HUMAN ADVENTURE by William McNamara, © Copyright 1991 William McNamara. Published by Element Books, Inc., Rockport, Massachusetts.

Page 52. Taken from THE MYSTERY OF CHRIST by Thomas Keating, © Copyright 1987 St. Benedict's Monastery. Published by The Continuum Publishing Company, New York, New York.

Page 60. Taken from PRAYER, STRESS AND OUR INNER WOUNDS by Flora Slosson Wuellner, © Copyright 1985 by The Upper Room. Published by The Upper Room, Nashville, Tennessee.

Page 70. Taken from THE SONG OF THE BIRD by Anthony de Mello, © Copyright 1982 by Anthony de Mello. An Image book, published by Doubleday of the Bantam Doubleday Dell Publishing Group, Inc., New York, New York.

Page 80. Taken from BREAKING BREAD by M. Basil Pennington, © Copyright 1986. Published by Harper & Row, San Francisco, California.

Page 90. Taken from THE SPIRITUAL GUIDE by Michael Molinos, © Copyright 1982 by Christian Books. Published by The Seedsowers, Christian Books Publishing House, Sargent, Georgia.

Page 98. Taken from PRACTICING THE PRESENCE OF GOD by Brother Lawrence, © Copyright 1982 by Whitaker House. Published by Whitaker House, Springdale, Pennsylvania.

Page 106. Taken from AWARENESS by Anthony de Mello, © Copyright 1990 by the Center for Spiritual Exchange. An Image book, published by Doubleday of the Bantam Doubleday Dell Publishing Group, Inc., New York, New York.

Page 116. Taken from MY UTMOST FOR HIS HIGHEST by Oswald Chambers, © Copyright 1935 by Dodd Mead & Co. Copyright renewed © 1963 by the Oswald Chambers Publications Association, Ltd. Published by Discovery House Publishers, Grand Rapids, Michigan.

Page 126. Taken from CENTERED LIVING by M. Basil Pennington, © Copyright 1986 BY CISTERCIAN ABBEY OF SPENCER, INC. An Image book, published by Doubleday of the Bantam Doubleday Dell Publishing Group, Inc., New York, New York.

Page 136. Taken from THE SACRAMENT OF THE PRESENT MOMENT by Jean-Pierre de Caussade, English translation © Copyright William Collins Sons & Co. Ltd., Glasgow 1981. Published by HarperCollins Publishers, New York, New York.

Page 148. Taken from SEEDS OF CONTEMPLATION by Thomas Merton, © Copyright 1961 by the Abbey of Gethsemani, Inc. Published by New Directions Publishing Corporation, New York, New York.

Union Life Ministries, Inc., is a not-for-profit corporation dedicated to an expanding awareness of God's "mystery...which is Christ in you."

We publish a bi-monthly magazine, *Union Life*, which emphasizes the liberating truths of our union in Christ, and God's passionate desire that we live in communion with Him.

Union Life is available without charge. Write to:

Union Life
P.O. Box 2877
Glen Ellyn IL 60138
Phone (630) 469-7757
FAX (630) 469-6731